Wisdom Beyond Me:
A Book of Messages about Living, Volume 1

Jeannie Bertoli, Ph.D.

©2014 Jeannie Bertoli

All rights reserved. Except for use in the case of brief quotations embodied in critical articles and reviews, the reproduction or utilization of this work in whole or part in any form by any electronic, digital, mechanical or other means, now known or hereafter invented, including xerography, photocopying, scanning, recording, or any information storage or retrieval system, is forbidden without prior written permission of the author and publisher.

The scanning, uploading, and distribution of this book via the Internet or via any other means without permission of the publisher and author is illegal and punishable by law. Purchase only authorized versions of this book and do not participate in or encourage electronic piracy of copyrighted materials. Your support of the author's rights is appreciated.

Names, characters, places, and incidents are based on the author's own personal experience therefore names of persons and entities remain unnamed to protect the integrity of the story and the privacy of those involved. Any group or organization listed is for informational purposes only and does not imply endorsement or support of their activities or organization.

For ordering, booking, permission, or questions, contact the author.

ISBN: 978-0-9912644-1-4

Printed in the United States of America by Create Space

Jeannie Bertoli

DEDICATION

This book is dedicated to all the Seekers, all those who sense within themselves that there is more to life. There is. May we find our way there together.

ACKNOWLEDGEMENTS

I would like to thank two people for their contributions to my life, and in helping this book come together. One is my long-time friend Diane Geisert who offered her keen eye and her time. She was instrumental when I needed it. The other is the person who has always supported and believed in my work, and the information contained in the book...Paul Ramsaroop. It was he who (years ago) insisted that I must publish these messages. Thank you both so much.

FOREWORD

Do you feel as though something is missing in your life? No matter how your life is filled or fulfilled, is there a part of you that longs for more, that feels as though something is not quite right or something is missing? If so, this book is for you. It is my belief that this type of feeling is a great gift from the Universe (or Spirit or God) that will not allow us to fully forget why we came to this life.

As much as we would like to lose ourselves within this lifetime, something doesn't quite allow it. There is a small (or big) feeling nudging us. It can be a poke, a pinch, or feelings of unhappiness, dissatisfaction or anxiety – however you experience it. For me, I experienced it as a slight depression.

I had a life that exceeded my dreams. I worked about 20 hours per week in a career that I loved and believed in strongly. I walked five blocks from my beautiful home in a community I loved to my beautiful office. I had plenty of money to do what I wanted to do and had wonderful friends with whom I enjoyed spending time. I lived in a beautiful city that I was overjoyed and proud to live in. And yet...

Something was missing. I think I was really surprised at first because I had put in all of this work, what I called investment years, in graduate school, moving, getting licensed, finding the right location, building a practice, honing my skills, finding and purchasing a home, etc. All of it took about 15 years. So here I was, with this amazing life that I had worked really hard to create, and yet, something was missing.

Of course, it was fantastic for a while and I reveled in the fact that the hard work was over and I had made it. I enjoyed the trappings of my success and felt great inside that I had persevered through many, many terrible and trying situations and circumstances and had made it to the other side. I was a success story; living the American dream of someone self-made, who had paid and paved her way. And, boy, it wasn't easy.

There were many painful, lonely times. Many situations I do not even want to re-visit in my mind now. Yet, I pushed through. I persevered and made it through the next step and the next and the next; determined to make it. For me, 'making it' was getting myself to a point where I could not work so hard. Invest, push and go; letting nothing stop me. Get to the finish line, then relax and have it relatively easy for the rest of my life. I don't know what your idea of success is but that was definitely mine.

So there I was; I had 'made it,' and after a while, it did not feel the same. The initial exhilaration and relief gave way to a little wondering. From that point on, I noticed that this life wasn't feeling as great as it had or as I had expected it to be. The feeling was just strong enough to make me say, "'Huh; that's interesting. That's not what I expected."

It probably won't surprise you that the feeling grew to a point where it was with me most days and felt like a slight depression. Here I was; I had scraped and crawled to create my dream life. I had not screwed up enough and was lucky enough not to have gone to jail or gotten into a bad marriage or had an unwanted pregnancy. I was done…and yet.

This book is for anyone who feels that nudging. No matter your path or how you experience it, you feel something is missing. You know somewhere inside you that life must be about something more. Something is not right.

If you talk to your friends or professionals about it, they may speak to you about anxiety or depression, or tell you everything is fine or will be fine once _____ happens. That blank may be getting through a current situation, finding a great love, getting a better job or some other outside circumstance. And you may wait until you have that thing and see that the feeling resolves only for a short time. Then, you are left wondering, "What else?"

If you're not paying close attention, you might not even notice the feeling. You might just be thinking about what needs to be changed or added to your life. Most of us were taught that when something doesn't feel good deep within us, we should look for an external solution. So, notice if you keep looking for the next solution, and the next, and the next. This may be in the form of trying to change others, circumstances, or yourself.

How would you complete this sentence, "I'd feel better if only _____."? My guess is that your answer will be about changing yourself, your partner or some major circumstance of your life. And for those of you who would change yourself, your answer is more likely to be that you need to lose weight or stop obsessing about something rather than, "I need to change **_how_** I live. Society got it wrong and my family got it wrong" (because they had also been indoctrinated by the norms of society).

This book is for all of you who resonate with this. Even if it is not a perfect fit, you know this is talking about you and how you feel.

This book is for all who hunger for more.

TABLE OF CONTENTS

WISDOM BEYOND ME:

WELCOME TO MY NEW START...AND HOW IT HAPPENED	13
HOW TO MAKE THE MOST OF THIS BOOK	17
ARE YOU WILLING?	19
PROLOGUE	21
TIME TO CLEAN HOUSE & MOVE INTO PEACE (PART ONE)	27
TIME TO CLEAN HOUSE & MOVE INTO PEACE (PART TWO)	34
GUIDANCE AWAITS YOU...NO ONE IS DENIED	40
THE JOURNEY WITHIN	46
ASK AND YOU WILL ALWAYS RECEIVE ANSWERS	52
PRODUCTIVITY AND PEACE THROUGH SIMPLICITY	58
PEACE IS ALWAYS AVAILABLE, BUT MUST BE CHOSEN	63
PROCESSES FOR REMOVING BLOCKS & MANIFESTING YOUR DESIRES	70
EMBRACE ALL OF YOU	76
FIND PEACE IN ONENESS WITH THE EARTH	82
ARE YOU READY TO FACE YOUR EXCUSES?	87
RELEASE YOUR GRIP ON WHAT IS & ALLOW FOR WHAT MAY BE	93
FACING OUR INCONSISTENCIES...FINDING PEACE	98
YOU ARE LOVED	105

HEALTH & ILLNESS (PART ONE)	108
HEALTH & ILLNESS (PART 2)	112
WHAT ARE YOU NUMBING?	116
WHAT WE BEAM OUT TO THE WORLD	125
"A BEAUTIFUL DETACHMENT"	131
THE POWER OF FEAR IN EVERYDAY LIFE	134
LOOK BEHIND THE CURTAIN	139
COME BACK TO THE NATURAL STATE	144
LETTING GO	151
FOR ALL THOSE WITH A CALLING	156
ARE YOU WILLING TO EXAMINE YOUR OWN HEART?	161
ALIGN YOURSELF WITH THE FLOW OF LIFE	168
MAKE THE MOST OF YOUR TIME HERE	172
HELPING PEOPLE TRANSITION & NOT OFFER A HOME FOR PAIN	177
LEARNING TO TRUST THROUGH LISTENING & ALIGNING	182
FREE YOURSELF FROM INDOCTRINATION	190
SEEK NOT SECURITY FROM EARTHLY THINGS	196
DREAM THE IMPOSSIBLE DREAM	203
SOAR!	207
CONTEMPLATION AND REALIGNMENT	212
LITTLE IS NEEDED FOR WHAT REALLY MATTERS	216

TIME FOR FUN AND A NEW FOCUS	**222**
THE SOUL LONGS TO HEAL ITS WOUNDS	**227**
NOTICING SOCIETAL BRAINWASHING	**233**
RECLAIMING YOUR ESSENCE	**240**
BREAKING INDOCTRINATION THROUGH CURIOSITY	**245**
BEGIN THE JOURNEY WITHIN	**251**
SEEK "OTHER WAYS OF KNOWING"	**257**
ALIGN WITH THE RHYTHMS OF LIFE	**263**
FOCUS ON YOU AND ASK SOME BIG QUESTIONS	**269**
A DEATH OF THE SOUL	**276**
THE TIPPING POINT	**283**
ALL YOU CAN REALLY DO FOR OTHERS AND WHAT YOU CAN DO FOR YOURSELF	**289**
RELEASE THE SEDIMENT	**295**
CONCLUSION	**301**
EPILOGUE	**302**

WELCOME TO MY NEW START... AND HOW IT HAPPENED

Welcome everyone to my first book! It is a compilation of messages I have received during my morning meditations.

Coming from a traditional background, I had not been exposed to people in direct communication with the spirit world. Now, I have the pleasure to be in communion with something (I'm not sure what) that is beyond myself. Through this interchange, I obtain direct feedback about my life as well as about life itself. The latter information is for all who wish access to it. I offer it to you now, freely, in this book.

You will be given a view into my life and my journey; full of foibles and some successes. I have fallen and gotten up, time and again. You may see yourself in some of my choices and in the lessons they give me. I offer you the words given to me so that you can see I am an ordinary person, no more special than anyone else.

I did not start this life as a spiritualist, do not have special psychic abilities and was not afforded more grace than anyone else. My mistakes far outnumber my successes, I am sure. Regardless, like many of you, I am proud of who I am and how I continue to progress and develop myself. I know many of you will hear these messages as though they were for you. I believe that is how it is meant to be. May they serve you well.

Immediately following the deaths of my dear uncle and my father, which occurred in quick succession, I found myself suddenly seeking the advice of spiritual readers. I had never done this or really believed in this before, but there I was.

The common theme in their feedback was that I had the ability to communicate with the spirit world (which I have come to believe we all do), and that I could and should begin doing so and writing the information I received. I was intrigued by the suggestion but had no idea where to begin.

After some initial resistance, I asked one of the readers to give me a process for doing this, as I had no idea where to begin. He gave me a specific meditation to do for five minutes and suggested I try "automatic writing." This meant that I would do the meditation and then sit in the silence with a pencil in hand, waiting for my hand to move.

Well, nothing impressive happened. I wound up with a bunch of pages of scribble. Then, I decided to switch to a laptop; just put my hands on the keys and see if information came to me (rather than my hands actually moving on their own). Thoughts did come; words did come. Soon enough, they were coming every time I sat down after quieting my mind through a specific meditation or silence or listening to drumming.

People have asked me what the source of this information is and I respond that I simply don't know. I can tell you what I sense and I can tell you what 'they' have told me (see 'They' Describe Themselves section in the Appendix). I realize, however, that this is not scientifically testable and there will be people who will immediately disregard these messages for that reason alone. I accept that.

I have also been asked how I know that this is not just my own thoughts coming together in a different way. Of course I can never be certain, but what I can tell you is this: Firstly, I do not speak in this manner in my life. I never have. The sentence structures and nomenclatures are simply not mine. Secondly, I have never had these thoughts previously and they do not represent information that I know. While I have studied many things in my life and read many books, I have never contemplated these messages and themes in the way they are presented to me in my meditation time.

I am also asked how I receive this information; how I hear it. While I find it really difficult to convey a metaphysical experience in 'regular' words, I will try. In a sense, it is that I hear information, but this is not an audible hearing, in that it doesn't come from outside my head in through my ears. It is more like thoughts that come just as regular thoughts do, which I just know, as much as we know anything, don't come from me. They come from a different source than my own brain. I experience it as, for example, my thoughts coming from a specific location in my brain and these coming from another, one with one voice (tone, speaking style, etc.) and one with another. I apologize that I cannot explain it better but this is the best I have come to so far.

I have previously shared some of my messages publicly in a blog; posting the messages anonymously under the pseudonym, "The Anonymous Spiritualist." I work in a very traditional field and hold degrees and licenses in arenas where some may not be comfortable with what I am saying here. Because of that, I was nervous as to how it (and I) would be received. Since then, I have grown to have the courage of my convictions and to know with all my heart that these messages are to serve mankind. Therefore, I now stand proudly, and publically, beside them.

Finally, I share with you my truth; that a Universe of support and love surrounds us constantly. We need only tap into it to feel and understand things normally not sensed or validated by a logic-based world.

Come explore with me the inner-workings of the Universe. May we enjoy the ride together!

- *Jeannie Bertoli* (aka The Anonymous Spiritualist)

HOW TO MAKE THE MOST OF THIS BOOK

It is my greatest hope that you will use this book to bring you closer to the essence of who you are, and bring you in communication with the Wisdom of the Universe. I want you to find that you are guided and supported by Universal forces, not through faith but through experience.

I recommend that you have a journal and, as you read each message, write down your thoughts. Note what catches your attention in the message, and what it makes you think about. Let your imagination be free to go wherever it wishes. Allow yourself to wander to new places and see what fun you can have. See what comes to you and how that changes as you make your way through the book.

EXERCISES

There are exercises and questions sprinkled throughout this book. Completing them will definitely enhance your experience. You may do so as you read, or mark them and return later when you are in the right space to dig in.

NOTE

Just a quick note about my writing style. It is not always grammatically correct – I use fragments, I use commas sometimes too little and sometimes extraneously, and I know that. I also sometimes make up words (that I think should be words) that are self-explanatory but not in the dictionary. I generally put them in quotes so that you know I know they are not proper words. Try it sometime. Make up your own words and use poetic license in writing style...it's fun!

ARE YOU WILLING?

"It is not the critic who counts; not the man who points out how the strong man stumbles, or where the doer of deeds could have done them better. The credit belongs to the man who is actually in the arena, whose face is marred by dust and sweat and blood; who strives valiantly; who errs, who comes up short again and again, because there is no effort without error and shortcoming; but who does actually strive to do the deeds; who knows great enthusiasms, the great devotions; who spends himself in a worthy cause; who at the best knows in the end the triumph of high achievement, and who at the worst, if he fails, at least fails while daring greatly, so that his place shall never be with those cold and timid souls who neither know victory nor defeat." - Teddy Roosevelt

PROLOGUE
'They' Describes Themselves

Before you begin the messages, here is some information about the messengers. This was a message in which they describe themselves. It may aid you in understanding the material to know where it is coming from, or at least my understanding of where it is coming from. Here, then, is 'them' describing themselves:

Today we are going to talk about meeting us. People will wonder, as they read this, how they can meet us and be in relationship with us. So we want to address this specific matter.

> ***You and we are all one.***

We come from one source. When each of us splits off and comes into form, we do not lose the tie to the rest and to The Whole. You cannot, no matter what you do, lose your connection to the rest of us, and The Whole, which some call God. You cannot be bad enough or mean enough, or even good or kind enough, to impact these relationships. They are not earned; the relationships are who you are.

This connection is not just with other people in form. In fact, that is the smallest portion of those to whom you are connected. You are connected to all other energy, which means all other things on your earth as well as all energy that is not bound to the earth. We are among those things not bound to the earth. We are energy not in form, which some call 'formless energy'.

In some ways we are no different from you. We are energy that is both individuated and connected with the ability to create and direct our 'lives', if you want to call them that. Really, as it is for you, we have the ability to direct our thoughts, emotions, and actions. We can organize them and offer them to the world in a certain trajectory with a specific intention and vibration. By vibration, we mean what you would call kindness or meanness. We can send things out with support, with callousness, etc.

Now the differences between you and us are that we do not send things out with various intentions, but always from a place of love and respect and compassion. On this plane, other emotions are no longer a part of our thinking or our existence. While that may sound like a relief to you, it is simply different. It is obtained when you have done that level of work, have raised your vibration and no longer seek to be in 'ego' (or whatever other word you would like to use for that). It is a many-lifetimes journey to even desire to let go of such matters and live in peace.

When you can live there in form while also living in peace and maintaining a high vibration around those who are otherwise, then you start to lift yourself away from lifetimes there in form, and toward lifetimes elsewhere, like where we are. By high vibration, we mean coming from pure intent –

offering love, peace, and compassion. Coming from pure intent means not seeking anything in return for what you put out in the world, having no attachment to what happens next but simply offering yourself with love.

We tell you all of this so that you may understand us better, and so we are not an elusive possibility. We are, in fact, your brothers and sisters in many ways, yet different in vibration and dimension. We are the same and different. It is our sameness that has us reach out to you. Most of us have gone through the path you now take and so we are especially able to assist you. There are also others who never took the world of form and are able to be of assistance in different ways, for they hold the highest levels of knowledge of the universe. They are the knowledge keepers and inform us all.

The people that guide you the most are those who have been where you are. You, JB, are even able to recognize some of the souls who once walked the earth, including your father and Chief Black Bear. Your father, who was hugely flawed and full of ego on earth, is now in a place of purity and knowledge. You can tell when you interact with him that he is the same soul, has the same personality, but is vastly different in other ways. He is full of love, as he always was, but it is pure love and not love clouded by matters of the ego and wounds that he never faced. Given all that he did and did not do, he may and will

likely choose to return there, but right now he is so happy being without those concerns. He is basking in life without form. He loves this version of himself that he can more easily choose here, without the distractions and temptations of life in form.

To begin to be in relationship with us, we wanted you to have a basis to know who we are. We are you, but with knowledge of all and purity of mind and spirit. There is a part of you that is that too, but it is far buried, deep within you. You must seek it in the silence. If you wish to connect with us, which will help you connect with that part of yourself, we are here. Simply listen for us in the silence. We are in the wind, in your heart, in the places easily overlaid by matters of the earth. We will continue to seek you and await your response.

Until then…we love you all.

Jeannie Bertoli

MESSAGES

TIME TO CLEAN HOUSE & MOVE INTO PEACE (PART ONE)

Good morning. Well it is a whole new year there. It is the beginning of many new things. It is not just another day on the calendar. These cycles mean something and do matter. This year is a year of action for you and for many others. Last year was a cycle of change, breakdown, and preparation. You did all of those things.

After many, many losses and then much time alone in contemplation and considering new information, you came out of the darkness and silence and are re-entering the world anew. You began this re-entry at the end of last year, but that was just getting over the precipice. It was the initial steps to get over fears and jitters.

Now as you enter this year, you will be challenged to live with full courage, to be out in the world and vocal and unafraid to express what you sense and believe. You sense much. You know much. You have been given much, entrusted with much.

What it takes from you now is an increasing willingness to be in that place and speak it from your heart, with humility and humanity, to be it and speak it without attachment to how it is received. You have nothing to lose. No one is going to burn you at the stake. You are already going to die. You have no community that will be lost. Your fears are only fears and not probabilities.

As you know, fear lives in the possibility, not the probability. Speaking out about living differently, more than mindfully, can still be done within your profession, within that box of 'legitimacy' within the world. It is time for you to speak out regularly when asked or when there is an opportunity. When with clients, bring them back to themselves, teach them to listen to themselves – less cognition and more heart.

> ***Now as you enter this year, you will be challenged to live with full courage, to be out in the world and vocal and unafraid to express what you sense and believe.***

Q: What will this year mean for the world and for humanity?
A: It will mean much. This is a big year of choices, of one trajectory or another. The level of systemic destruction that has taken place can destroy society and humanity if drastic change does not take place. Already much has been set into motion due to greed and other maniacal forces. There is darkness, a 'woundedness' that has set systems into motion.

Then there is also what we have been telling you about, regarding incrementally worse systems. This is where, like in lobbying, something that started out as a good or certainly not bad idea got incrementally and slowly worse with single actions that expanded the realm of what was possible.

So one day someone took a congressman to lunch, and then that was acceptable to the system. And one day, a lobbyist asked a legislative favor and got it, and that was acceptable. And the same with campaign contributions for favors. So once these things were initiated and became acceptable, they became prolific. Then once they were mainstays, the next expansive idea was introduced. Soon enough the system was 'bad' enough, meaning far enough away from the original values, that it would have been better to sweep it clean, using the original values as a standard for rebuilding.

You saw this in the documentary about Broadway. They said every 20 years a new cycle began and what Broadway was, was redefined. Forgetting the timeframe, periodically systems at every level need to be swept clean. The house needs to be emptied and then refilled with a renewed sense of what this place means and what it values. Whether you agree with the new definition of values or not is irrelevant, as you can choose to participate in its next iteration, or not.

This is very important information for you to pass on, for it is true for everyone on every level. It is true at the cellular level for each person, and upward and outward from there. It is true for every person in every part of their lives, and out to the largest systems.

Without you knowing, this is done in the ecosystems of nature. Forests burn and renew. Seasons bring renewal and re-choosing of what returns. For people it is important in your job, your relationships, your routines, your physical home, your own self (thoughts and personal ways of being), your communities, etc.

Your society has come away from valuing this renewal and re-choosing, but it is what (you may see) creates a ridding of what is no longer viable or valuable, and a place for new growth.

EXERCISE:
- *How am I living?*
- *What matters to me about this?*
- *If I wiped the slate (of my life) clean and just put back what I value most, what would return?*
- *What do I value most?*
- *What is life about?*
- *What have I come to know?*

- *If I look only at where I spend my time, what would it say I value?*
- *If I look only at where I spend my money, what would it say I value?*

Think about this as a literal exercise. Let us take the example of your job.

If you had no job, what kind of job would you select based on your personal values and what it means to you to work?

If you value making money and making a contribution, what would that mean?

If you value working for a company that shares your values, what would that mean?

Why would you work for a company that didn't share your values?

Do you really believe there's any short-cut in that?

What the company values is what is passed on and offered to the employees – nothing more, nothing less. You cannot 'get away' with having your values without absorbing those of the company. If a company is taking from the earth, you cannot be a part of that company without being a part of taking from the earth. There is no 'getting away with' anything. It doesn't matter what other people think or what mask you are able to wear.

There is a truth about why you do what you do; there is no escaping it. You cannot escape yourself. This applies to every intention, every action in your life.

> *Your society has come away from valuing this renewal and re-choosing, but it is what (you may see) creates a ridding of what is no longer viable or valuable, and a place for new growth.*

Jeannie Bertoli

TIME TO CLEAN HOUSE & MOVE INTO PEACE (PART TWO)

You can't run from yourself...and that's good news. This is really good news.

So since you're not getting away with anything, you might as well live from your heart, heal your wounds, give to your earth, and give to your community. There is no other whole second existence where rationalizations mean anything other than pretense.

Defenses and rationalizations only create a *very* thin façade. One small scratch from a knowing place and the ridiculousness falls away. Since you cannot get away with anything, you may as well be honest...in everything, every matter, every instance. You may as well face the result of cheating on this or hating that person. You may as well be honest, because you are getting away with **nothing**.

This also ties back into 'cleaning house' as we described earlier. This is one technique that occurs as things swell beyond their usefulness – the rationalizations are in place. Let's take spending as an example. "I spend too much because: I have children, I am too tired to cook, everyone does, the banks solicited me knowing I couldn't pay, I work really hard, you only live once, I deserve to be happy...etc."

Now when you empty your financial house and begin again, remove all these excuses and begin with what you value, what matters to you and why. So many people spend much more money than they need to with justifications about wanting to make their children happy. You may see by now that this feeds into rationalizations about parenting. 'Wanting to make your children happy' is about you and not about parenting.

> ***Since you're not getting away with anything, you might as well live from your heart, heal your wounds, give to your earth, and give to your community.***

This is a separate complex issue, but parenting can be about many things from just getting your children to adulthood (alive and out of the house), to having a value system where they contribute to the world, to teaching them to be grounded in themselves with peace and joy and love.

Again, wipe the slate clean. Ask yourself: What is the role of a parent – what do you think? Go with what you value. Of course you want your children to be happy people, but children's ways are fickle and if you run around trying to make them happy in this moment or that, you will spend all your time doing that...and that is not the role of a parent to most. What do you think the role of a parent is? Align your actions with your answer.

So this was all to answer your question about what the year will bring. It is the end of these bloated systems and the needed house-cleaning will begin to occur. This can and should occur at every level of everyone's lives and with the systems all around. Those who are on the leading edge can be doing this in their own lives with diligence.

This is what we have been encouraging you to do. Have clean, efficient systems of pure intent. Hide nothing. Face fears. Take that hard look in the mirror and face yourself. Deal kindly with those around you. Apologize where you need to. Retract your energy from others' business and tend to your own. Make them pure; come back to the values of compassion for others.

Have your goals be a focus on love, joy, peace, and service. The more you clean out all that is 'other' than that, the more pure and nimble you will be for what lies ahead. This is like cleaning out your eyes so that you might see clearly. If you 'see' clearly, there is much you will see before others see it.

While we are saying 'see' it, we really mean that you sense it, but this is hard to describe in your words because it is not an accepted, regular input and influence. Think of it as regularly checking in with your instincts. Not 'what do I feel' but 'what do I sense'. See if you can tap into what 'seems' to be going on, whether that is someone's mood or whether they are telling you the truth. Begin tapping into this other form of information that is available to you in every moment. You can notice things before others and be prepared to adjust your life accordingly. Those who are still living in rationalizations may be destroyed by their own denials.

The message to all of you is the same: clean out your own house at all levels, face all fears and rationalizations, become as pure and clean and efficient as you possibly can, live from love. We say this not to scare you. You need the information but it cannot come from a place of fear. Do these things because you know they are long overdue and because it is the true calling of your heart. You need no other reason.

We will leave you with that today. Remember that you are loved and guided and need only seek our assistance. We will always be here for you, for all of you.

> *The message to all of you is the same: clean out your own house at all levels, face all fears and rationalizations, become as pure and clean and efficient as you possibly can, live from love.*

Jeannie Bertoli

GUIDANCE AWAITS YOU...
NO ONE IS DENIED

Good morning all. It is a wonderful day today, a day of openings, of possibilities, of new opportunities. Keep your mind open and a focused alertness. New ideas, new thoughts, new opportunities will be coming your way, not just this day but in the days to come. If you are simply in the moment and open, you will hear them and see them for what they are.

JB: There is such a strong energy today pulling me into such a deeply altered state. It is almost overwhelming. I know there is some important message here, something very important. I only hope I can transmit it.

Yes, the strength of energy has increased, partially because of the importance and partially because you can take it now. You are so much purer in your intent that we can increase the frequency by which we communicate with you.

The important message is the bugler announcing to people to pay attention. The time is near; the time has come. All those who are sleeping, arise from your slumber. Wipe the sleep from your eyes and awaken. The time is at hand. Change has come. Your opportunity has arrived. The new day is here.

It is time to throw away convention and follow your heart. Leave the expectations of others behind you; shed the weights that once bore down on you. Come into a period of light and see not limitations. The time of opening and opportunity has arrived.

To do this, begin by stopping and listening. Be alert. Be ready. Anticipate each moment and what wisdom and guidance will come across your path.

You, JB, are doing this often. You see possible signs and omens in what people say and what they do not say. A friend mentions a thought and you wonder if that thought was for you and the Universe used that friend to transmit it to you. You are listening intently, awaiting the opening, awaiting the sign. This is very important.

> ***There is no time that you will not be guided if you simply ask for guidance and then create the space for it to come.***

You also can and should state intentions and be increasingly in co-creation. You want to move. You know this place is not a home for you. It is time. Co-create the opening for a new home where you can lay down roots, build community, and stay. Find the place, energetically, where your energy fits.

Co-create it with intention and attention. Find others with whom your values align but also expand your thinking.

As for the rest of you, follow this process for whatever you wish to create. Be focused; pay attention; be intentional. Sit in silence and deep peace and decide what you would like to create that is aligned with the laws of nature, the Universe (God/Nature), and the purpose of your life.

This is not difficult to do if you take the time to do it. Be with yourself...and be with us.

There is no other way. There is no complicating factor. There is no time that you will not be guided if you simply ask for guidance and then create the space for it to come.

You need only be ready and enact this simple process. Do that and you will never be denied. Those who would say they 'tried' and nothing came are fooling themselves. There is no other way. We would never deny you. We are a group of souls/guides/entities/angels devoted to your service. We are honored to be as such.

We await the chance to be of service, and it would and will never be otherwise. You shall not call out into the wilderness and hear no reply. We are with you and here for you. That is how it shall ever be.

Call on us; we invite you. Seek our council. All those who fear that they are alone, who think The Universe or God has abandoned you – we promise you, it cannot be true. Call out to us and we shall reply.

We are excited this day to sound the drum to all people. There is no one forgotten, no one unworthy. All are welcomed into the kingdom. Come sit by our side and commune. Together we will love and spread light.

When filled with light, you seek only to spread it. Nothing else matters. Beaming light, being of service; this is all that matters. Being and sharing love in the world is all there is. All else fades away and pales in comparison.

Come fill yourself up. Sit with us in the glory of oneness.

Temporarily depart from your earthliness and feel the vibration of total peace, total joy, and a state with no concerns. Once you touch that place and feel it within you, you understand things you never understood before. You understand all that matters.

As long as you are in that state, you truly understand everything. From that point on, as long as you re-enter or remember that state and integrate it into your life, you are altered and will never again be the same. Be love; beam love. It is a state of total bliss. May you touch it and be it often and find yourself glad of it, glad to be changed, glad to be lifted.

Amen, and amen.

> *No other 'thing' – money, power, relationship – can fill you up like the light of the world.*

Jeannie Bertoli

THE JOURNEY WITHIN

Good morning. We are with you today and glad you are here. You hear the first birds chirping in your backyard and it makes you smile. The worst of winter is ending and new life, spring, begins. It is a time for the old to fall away, for what has held you back to do so no longer. Yes, you were indoctrinated into your family and your society, probably more than you will ever know, but a full inventory of such things is not necessary for you all to move past them. And you must move past them to create exactly the kind of life and character you wish for yourself. By character we mean your values, and actions aligning with those values.

No longer should you be blinded by the ways around you in which you were raised. You must detach from those things and create anew.

EXERCISE:

Ask yourself:
- *Who are you?*
- *What does it mean to be you?*

- *What are the essential characteristics within you that you are most proud of and that make you feel most deeply peaceful and at home?*

Whatever those are, come back to them as the center of your life, as your nucleus. Let all else stem from those things. Let your actions then reflect what you know. No one else can tell you these things; no one can teach you how to be the best you. This is a journey within. Go within and sit with these questions. The answers are all there when you remove the distractions.

Of course people can help you on this journey and be with you in this process to go within. There will be mentors and guides and therapists who are of pure intent and are a source of great support on this journey. Utilize these services as it serves you. They often help you stay grounded and on-track, as the world still plays a large role in your life. Once down the path they are less needed, as the light within you is so bright that it cannot be disturbed.

You, JB, wanted to find someone to lead your journey. You for so long searched for and clung to leaders and mentors and communities that were on similar journeys or who could teach you or show you the way. You so much wanted a mentor, to be a protégé to someone you respected, just to follow in his or her steps. But that is not how it is meant to be and so was not so for you.

Following someone else's path is not the way to peace...to enlightenment. When you seek to follow, if you are aware, it shall not last long and you shall leave disappointed. This is the way of it. You are not meant to follow. You are not meant to follow someone else's journey or path.

The journey is yours, to go within and seek not an answer outside yourself. By going within, you will receive all the guidance and answers you desire and more. You will find love beyond measure, support without bounds. These are not things available in the outside world. You will only be disappointed if you seek them there.

> ***True and abiding peace and joy are possible, even on this planet in this time, in your bodies and in your lives.***

The most a teacher can do for you is continually show you a process, a path within yourself. Having gone that way themselves, they know a way in and can be with you as you ask the questions. They can help as you get the first answers and struggle with how to integrate the new you into a world filled with people who have not gone through such changes. That is a journey worth engaging in with a teacher or mentor or community or therapist. On this journey, you will find all the answers you ever sought. You will find clarity you did not even know was possible. True and abiding peace and joy are possible, even on this planet in this time, in your bodies and in your lives.

Of course as you change, you will change the circumstances of your life, but these are not requirements from anyone or anything outside of yourself. Simply, as you change, you set up your life differently. When you come from a place of peace, all that is not of peace is less appealing to you. As you come from a place of deep and pure joy, things that are otherwise will be less interesting, be they within your own thoughts or your surroundings, and so they will not continue to be chosen or focused upon.

If the thought of changing and your circumstances changing scares you, it is only because you know not how deeply peaceful and joyful you will feel. These things to which you cling – a house, a relationship, a job, etc. – they are substitutes for what we offer. The essence of your soul needs nothing else.

Let that fear be a warning sign that you are clinging to earthly things as if they matter. You are attributing to them the feelings of security and peace to the degree that you have them. But this is false. We offer you a way to a deep and abiding peace that cannot be removed, even through death.

It is time to come back to your essences, come back to yourselves. Be sure to do so with those who are of pure intent.

Listen and feel. You will know them.

Amen.

> *When you come from a place of peace, all that is not of peace is less appealing to you. As you come from a place of deep and pure joy, things that are otherwise will be less interesting.*

Jeannie Bertoli

ASK AND YOU WILL ALWAYS RECEIVE ANSWERS

Good morning. We are glad you are here today. What an interesting day, with some stolen time. Today will be a good day. It is an important time for you to stay on track. You have eaten so well and exercised despite feeling relatively unwell this week. Now that you no longer have your houseguest around, it is important to continue that level of self-care, most importantly because you love it. You love how it makes you feel; you love the concept of it. You love how clean and strong your body feels even though the air in this city does not work for you.

We know you want to move and are ready for that change to begin today. We want to acknowledge that you are done with this location and have decided to move on. You are awaiting a sign or an opportunity to present itself so you will know where and how to go. We honor that you are not just going to move again without these indicators. You could, of course, do this a third time in the last 18 months and then narrow from there. But we know you want roots and are committed to a different process. This is a process of listening and aligning. So right now you are in the listening phase. Ask your questions and listen for answers.

JB: Where will I move to next?

Answer: I (JB) feel pulled toward mid to southern California or Mexico just below California.

JB: What will bring me there and how will I know the specific place to go?

Answer: You will know. It will be revealed to you. All will be revealed and known. You need not figure it out in your head. You do not need to live like that anymore, with that pressure. We are here to support you and will show you all as it unfolds.

JB: While all of that makes sense to me, I am having a difficult time living here, physically, and don't want to continue living in this altitude and in this place of limbo.

> **You are always surrounded by support and love. To feel it, to enter it, to hear the answer you seek, you need only come into silence and release the things of the earth.**

Answer: We know. We know. It will be soon. And know that as long as you are there, there is much to learn. There always is. Wherever you are, we bring teachings to you. So *seek them; focus on them. You have enough to focus on to fully occupy yourself until the time comes. Focus on these things and not on what the next step will be. It will be, soon enough, and you will know it immediately, of course. In the meantime enjoy what is here and progress on your business and socialize with the locals.*

For the rest of you, JB's situation is one you can apply to whatever you are waiting for in your own lives. Many of you are looking for something or someone to change in your life. You look forward to the day when that 'thing' will be different, whether it is the addition of something new or the removal of something no longer wanted.

Use this same process. Be where you are. Know that the universe is surrounding and supporting you at all times. While you are waiting, focus on what you can learn, what you can do, how you can grow – in the circumstances you are in. Now we do not mean that some of you should not change your circumstances...you should. You know who you are. If you ask the question within about what action you should be taking – listen for the answer and align yourself with your deepest knowing.

JB is someone who acts so frequently, she needs to slow down to listen and align. Many others, as you listen and align, need to take action. It takes only a few honest moments in silence, without defenses, and the answers are clear. Which category are you in? Where do you need to act? Where do you need to stay still and learn what is here, and not act? Sit in silence and go deeply within. You will know.

If you are ever unsure about anything, ask us. We will always answer. If you do not hear us, continue to practice asking and then sitting in a deep place of listening. This is not a matter of 'trying' or 'trying harder'. It is your birthright and cannot be given or taken away. You are always surrounded by support and love. To feel it, to enter it, to hear the answer you seek, you need only come into silence and release the things of the earth.

Release your concerns, your thoughts, your fears. We do not dwell in those things. Like a conveyor belt, place those things outside of yourselves to be removed for the time being. Listen to toning or drumming, or nothing if you wish. Come to a place beyond the earth and we are there.

We are not in the place of thoughts, fears, and worries. We are outside of that and beyond that. You may access us at any time, for we are everywhere. Even when you are in a state of earthly worry – you may switch to us and access us. You can leave the earthly dimension to interact with us, then go right back. It is a matter of focusing your attention on one thing or another.

Have you ever looked at the time of day and seen one aspect of it, like how long you have been in the car, then a few moments later asked yourself what time it was and realized because you had been focused on what it meant in one context, you hadn't noticed that same piece of information for a different context? This is the same thing. There is so much around you at all times. So much that could be your focus, so many different opportunities for your attention. When you narrow in on one, you cannot narrow in on others; it is impossible.

So when you narrow in on the earthly moment, you exclude a focus on us – a choice you may re-make in every moment. If you shift your attention to us, you can then have that experience. Once you have established a relationship with us and know what that feels like, this is possible. Whenever you are ready, we are ready. We await you with love.

Blessings to you all this day.

Jeannie Bertoli

PRODUCTIVITY AND PEACE THROUGH SIMPLICITY

Good morning. We are glad you are here. Today you asked a question in your meditation and you received your answer. Now we want to share that with others. You asked for all anxiety and worry to be removed from your mind and your heart. You awoke in the middle of the night concerned about a few matters in your life. And you had dreams that contained worry. Though you woke up fine and in a great mood, you seek to end these elements in your life. You wish to be freed of the burden of worry or concern. You know that within this life, centered on spirit, there is no need for worry, and you want that reflected more greatly in your life. Most specifically, you do not want to be hard on yourself anymore, constantly pushing yourself and wishing you had done more. You want an ease and joy and peace through the day that does not have that pressure.

Whether or not others of you have these same desires, you can place your own concerns here and the answers will be the same.

Your answer came clearly...simplicity. Stay in a deeper space and float through a simple, organized day. Have a routine that meets your needs for productivity, fun, relaxation, etc. Then within that routine, rest and float through your day. In the schedule you have assured that you will be on track with your goals and aligned with your values. You know that what is important to you is accounted for. And so you may simply be in a place of joy and float within that routine.

Keep it simple and not overly-scheduled. The idea being, of course, that as you value peace, so it shall be in your routine. You need not schedule early morning to late in the night if you want peace. Prioritize and allow for rest, relaxation, recreation, socialization, nutrition, movement, and productivity.

> *Have a routine that supports your life and your deepest values, then float within it for the greatest peace. There is no need for chaos.*

Keep food simple, money simple, exercise simple. The idea being that when you remove the rush and pressure, you help remove the emotional elements from all of these.

So many eat as an indulgence rather than what is best for them, or spend in that way, or drink in that way. When you come back to simplicity and remove the chaotic pace and the chaotic mind, things become much simpler and without needing to meet an emotional vacuum. Go for a walk; feel the sun shine on your face. Laugh with a friend for hours. Walk your dog. Be in a place of peace.

Have a routine that supports your life and your deepest values, then float within it for the greatest peace. There is no need for chaos.

If you find yourself arguing with this message, you may wish to look within to see why. What would you have to give up to believe this? Some people are so entrenched in the chaos; they are almost addicted to it. Though it wears them out and drains their lives, they continue and feel as though it is necessary.

If they were to admit they could have their goals met without it, they would have to really question why they were doing it all along. They protect its necessity in order not to question themselves or realize that it was never necessary. We sympathize with the difficulty therein but encourage you to just take this in and realize that the sooner you choose otherwise, the happier the rest of your life can be.

Yes, you will have to face the questions as to why you created it to begin with, but you will be on a road to healing and a path to a better life. Those are wonderful rewards. Some people do not know how to live without the chaos; they have forgotten what life was like before.

Unwinding this adrenaline-based life and coming to a more thoughtful, considered place takes courage and focus, and a willingness to be wrong and face that egoic adjustment. We acknowledge that. For those of you who are ready, we will be with you each moment to support you and guide you. And if you need several tries before you are ready, that is wonderful too. We honor your desire, your efforts, your journey.

Blessings to you all.

PEACE IS ALWAYS AVAILABLE, BUT MUST BE CHOSEN

Good morning. We are glad you are with us today. Today is another good day. We know you have not been feeling well with all the headaches and difficulty breathing at this altitude. Know that you will find and settle in a home where these things are not an issue. It will not be long now and you will have a home space that supports your physical and mental health. While some would say that you could or should do more to accommodate to this location, it is not true. You are listening to your body and your mind and your experience and deciding if this place is a good fit for you, and you have experienced a very definite 'no'. While you have had a few positive signs, they quickly get drowned out by the confusing or uncomfortable. While this place is beautiful, it does not match your energy and does not feel good to you. You will soon find a place that is a great match for you, and we are excited for these coming days and times.

In the meantime, as we went over in detail yesterday, keep life simple and easy. Keep your mind without concern and without worry. Keep aligning your life with your goals and keep progressing in your business and expanding your experiences. Soon you will have more and more experiences and openings.

We will not say more than that – only be aware and be in a state of wonder as doors open. Be only conscious and you will see what comes to you. You were very touched yesterday when a friend came out of nowhere to offer you help with this transition. All will become clear on the role he may play. He is open and excited to be of assistance. The reality may or may not work out, but enjoy his offer for what it is, a desire to reach out to you and connect with you and make a contribution in your life. How beautiful. Savor that.

> *Peace is a whisper on the wind, that tiny hum or ohm, offering you her outstretched hand. She awaits you at all times and offers you herself completely.*

Now on to other matters. Today we want to talk to you all about peace. What brings peace? How can one attain it? The fact is that peace is all around you at all times, surrounding you and offering you her comfort. But she is not the only one around you, not the only offering. She is a whisper on the wind, that tiny hum or ohm, offering you her outstretched hand. Peace is a whisper on the wind, that tiny hum or ohm, offering you her outstretched hand. She awaits you at all times and offers you herself completely.

She will never become huge and fight for your attention. You must stop, create a space of silence, and listen for her. She awaits you at all times and offers you herself completely. You need only stop, get quiet, and choose her.

The louder voices are the energy of chaos, worry, anger, and fear. These hold very different vibrational fields. Their frequencies are such that they will be in your face and grab your attention. Like the quadrants from Stephen Covey's book, 7 Habits of Highly Effective People, peace is in the Important But Not Urgent quadrant, and chaos, worry, etc. are in the Urgent But Not Important. Worry, etc. will be in your face trying to demand your attention while peace will never be, and will always require you to affirmatively prioritize it.

When you realize that peace is a choice you make and not something that will fight for you, you may shift your thinking and expectations. Many, many people pray for peace, but do not do what is necessary to create it.

Peace is always a choice that is in alignment with your highest good. Create peace, select peace, offer peace. You can come into a state of peace where nothing else matters. JB can feel this right now. She is awash in it. All that you desire at that point is to maintain that glorious feeling. Know, also, that she must re-choose peace when she is feeling something otherwise. She is no different and there is not a time when you will only feel peace because you live in a world where there is contrast, where there is every available feeling.

Of all the things that you think you want in life, this feeling is really all you desire. Within this feeling, there is nothing but purity and joy and peace. You feel nothing else and offer nothing else to the Universe. It is a constant state of a low-level bliss.

The more you can touch this place, the more you have access to this place, the more you can experience this place, the more you can offer it to others. We keep emphasizing offering it to others because service is a part of life and because whatever state you are in, you automatically beam out to everyone else. There is no other way.

So no matter your internal state, you are offering that to the world entire. For some that may be an incentive to become more peaceful, but the best incentive is how it feels to experience this and to live as much as possible in that state.

It is from that state that your dreams can come true. From this state of purity and light, you may learn to manifest your desires that align with Life. From this state, there is a purity in your intent and your desired manifestations shift; they are based in peace. Once you experience this, you realize it is all that matters, and much else falls away.

On another note, there are many books and offerings on how to manifest things in your life using The Law of Attraction and other terms and phrases. This is a complicated matter. Selecting your desired outcomes and willing them into creation can happen, but it is much more complicated than would appear based on these books, speeches and movies. The calculus for what you are able to manifest is not yet really known or discussed by most. Know that it is not as simple as wishing for it and pretending like it is already true. On the other side, it is absolutely possible to influence what you manifest.

The difference is that there are many other factors other than the ones acknowledged by this genre of material. There is a whole life plan; there are reasons for which you chose this lifetime. And you have free will. All of these are true alongside that which is already taught.

The thing missing from all of this is listening and aligning with your deeper knowing about your life. Deciding you want a new Porsche and going about manifesting it may possibly work, but there are other factors at play. There are many other forces at work, both within your higher consciousness and the universal consciousness.

In your life, you have contracts and agreements and while you have free will at every level of consciousness and can choose otherwise, most people do not know how to do this. Be in the silence; be in a deep state of awareness and consciousness. From here you see a different life and listen to what is possible. Create from there and see what comes of it.

Blessings to you all.

> ***Many, many people pray for peace, but do not do what is necessary to create it.***

Jeannie Bertoli

PROCESSES FOR REMOVING BLOCKS & MANIFESTING YOUR DESIRES

Good morning. We are glad you are here today. What an amazing time this is in your life, and for the life on your planet. There are so many doors opening, so many new ideas, new opportunities. It is a glorious time to be alive if you are ready to be open and blossom. There have been few other times in history with this level of opening. It is at the energetic level that things are open.

There is expansion, opening, invitation, opportunity. There aren't even enough words in English to talk about this kind of reverse vortex. You may expand way beyond what you had thought possible in earthly ways and in spiritual ways. You may have success in relationships, business, physical activities (sports) in ways you never thought possible. Additionally, you may have spiritual experiences and abilities you never thought possible. It is a time for all these openings.

To take advantage of these things, you need only have focus and desire. With those two things, all is possible. If you are ready to begin remote viewing, be in a place of focused intent, ask for assistance, and you will begin to do it. If you wish to have more clients, the same is true. And on and on.

This is not done in a superficial way; it is a deep place of pure intent and groundedness. You cannot simply stay in your head and say you want this or that. But from a deep, grounded place, open your energy in expansion with open arms and state your intention from a place of providing a product or service and offering it to the world...and people will come. It can be no other way. When you offer your heart and the manifestation of that expression of heart through your work, and you declare its offering to the universe, it will be received and reverberated back.

> ***If you really want to become responsible, you can begin to really look at your thoughts and see how much of your life you have slowly and perhaps unwittingly turned over to other people.***

You, JB, do this every day for five minutes for a month and see what happens. See what 'miracles' will come. And for you, all of you, think of the relevant thing in your life that you want. Notice what blocks you may have around that desire. Do you desire more money but have a deep-seeded belief that only bad people get money? Do you want to lose weight but have some voice that says it is not possible? If you have these or other blocks, those must first be removed.

You cannot do the earlier offering until these blocks have been removed. You cannot be in pure intent as long as you have these blocks. It is a mixed message and the universe will reflect back that mixed message.

How you remove those blocks is by being in a process similar to the offering ritual, but in releasing. First, you must acknowledge that you have a block; define it as clearly as you can. Spend some time making this identification and do not rush through it in an attempt to get the answer or the results. The time you take to be in this process will be reflected in the results. We do not mean time itself so much but non-anxious, non-frenetic, considered, grounded time in contemplation. Ask yourself: What other thoughts do I have about this issue? What possible things may be blocking me?

This is not 'what excuses do I have'? It is deeper than that. What are the blocks that cause me to point to my rationalizations/excuses? "I don't have time" is an excuse for many people regarding many issues. That is not the block. The block is the thing that causes you to say that excuse and points to it, rather than a solution.

You all have excuses for why you do not have different things in your life that you want. It's your spouse's fault, because of the city you live in, your boss, the people around you, your genetics, lack of time, because you have children, or anything else. Step one is to realize that none of these is true.

You do not have what you wish in your life because of you. The moment you stop feeling oppressed by the outside force of your excuse, you can begin to realize that you are in charge and powerful and whatever limitations your life has are because of you and your choices. I choose not to travel more because I have a dog and don't want to leave her alone any more. I choose not to make more money because this job provides me a sense of security right now, even though I know nothing is really secure and things could change at that job and then I might feel devastated and blame them for 'taking away' 'my' job or security, which I pretend like they were in charge of. If you really want to become responsible, you can begin to really look at your thoughts and see how much of your life you have slowly and perhaps unwittingly turned over to other people, and then held them responsible, without their consent by the way. You blame bosses and children and spouses for how you feel and how you act...prolifically.

There is a real opportunity here and now to change these patterns, clear up these excuses, these stories, find the blocks beneath them, clear those and move on in POWER! What an opportunity! Take back your lives! This time, more than ever in your lives, the universe is open to support you, like the wind at your back. Make the smallest efforts and you will see it is not as difficult as you thought, and it is truly not as difficult as it was if you tried to face this in the past.

Now is the time. Seize the opportunity. Make your way. In this realm, there is power and beauty and freedom. We await you.

> ***This time, more than ever in your lives, the universe is open to support you, like the wind at your back.***

Jeannie Bertoli

EMBRACE ALL OF YOU

Good morning. We are glad you are here. Today we want to talk to you about peace and balance. Peace is the key to enjoying your life in this form. And balance is the key to your peace. Try not to think of these terms as they are currently used by your society. Instead, we offer you a new idea of balance. Balance for us is that acceptance of all: no one right answer and no one wrong answer. No dichotomy, no this or that, but a 'balance' of both. This is true whether masculine and feminine, hard or soft, kind or cruel. Think of things no further as opposites but as the whole. You are the whole and you are all of these characteristics.

Finding peace is a matter of being your whole expression, which is a balance of all these characteristics. You are generous and selfish. You do not want to be too much of one and not enough of the other. Think of this visually as a globe spinning this way and that in a beautiful slow flow. You are this and that, and this and that. You are all of it, or it would not all be within you. You are so beautiful exactly as you are.

You have been taught that some of these characteristics are 'good' and others 'bad'. Some should be encouraged and others extinguished. We say to you otherwise today. To do as you have been taught is to deny yourself. There is a reason all characteristics were put in you and exist within you today. This means not selecting one characteristic and displaying that disproportionately, a specific characteristic whether you think of it as 'good' or 'bad'.

We want you to know today that you are all of it. You are the entire host of characteristics and that is how it should be. You are strong and weak, tough and vulnerable. Illness often comes from trying to be one of these and not the other, or at least minimizing the experience of one, like vulnerability. There is great joy in the acceptance of all of it and the willingness to allow all of it to flow through you.

> *Yes, you will have raging, murderous moments. And if you are living in a place of flow and acceptance of all, they will soon abate.*

You are a whole creature. There is amazing joy in allowing the expression of that wholeness rather than some selected sub-section. When you do that you deny yourself, which leads to myriad problems and cover-ups and illnesses, much like a lie that builds upon itself and requires a whole system just to sustain that lie.

We know this is a lot to take in because many of you will immediately think of the characteristics that you are not or do not wish to be. We understand it will be a transition and a process to begin to let this concept be considered rather than rejected outright. We invite you into the process of consideration.

Allow yourselves to feel what it would be like to be in the flow of this acceptance of all – resisting nothing but allowing your mind and heart to feel the full expression of your being. You are jealous and you are angry, and you are so amazingly kind and generous. You are all of it, and we hope you come to see that denying any of it only brings you to a place of suppression and rejection (*JB: I am given the feeling of holding my breath*).

There are some of you who will be ready to release that breath and live in freedom. In that freedom there is peace, great peace.

Now we know many will have the immediate question of what will happen if we allow ourselves the space to experience all the things we currently suppress (all the 'negative' emotions like cruelty, fury, jealousy, rage – all the 'scary' ones). So let us just tell you now that your fear of these is what has given them such big words and power in your language and lives. Yes, you will have raging, murderous moments. And if you are living in a place of flow and acceptance of all, they will soon abate. The same is true of the greatest words you have for the other side of the spectrum. When you feel the greatest forms of joy and love, and experience those, they soon abate.

We are talking about the full expression of your mind and your body, your form. By allowing your internal life to be a full and complete expression, without suppression, you will also be in a place to see that you do not need to cling to any of these things and thereby stop the flow.

These things flow in and they flow out. You allow them to do what they were meant to do – flow in, flow out. Emotions are here to teach you about yourself, not to be attached to, clung to, or even ever acted upon. They are showing you yourself.

When you cling and attach or try to stop the flow of the whole, you can see by now that you cause the same problems for yourself. You are trying to stop life from being what it is. You like a certain feeling and try to cling to it so that it won't leave. Like the lie, a whole system is then created to support that clinging, all of which is against the flow of life. It is not sustainable without cutting off your experience and creating other symptoms, like a ripple through the water.

Many of you can see this with ease today. Take this in to the degree that you are able. And re-read it as you wish, for it is important and may take you much time to absorb. We are here with you always; embrace the seeker within you. Know that all of you are supported always, and that this message is not finished today but will continue.

Blessings to all.

> *Emotions are here to teach you about yourself, not to be attached to, clung to, or even ever acted upon. They are showing you yourself.*

Jeannie Bertoli

FIND PEACE IN ONENESS WITH THE EARTH

Good morning. We are so glad you are here child. There is much to say today. We are excited today to talk to you about living in oneness. You were shown and given the experience of something this morning during your meditation that we are excited to now put into words for others. Why don't you start to describe it and then we will take it from there?

JB: Sure. I was taken by this ancestor, a wise man who looked like a Native American (or some kind of indigenous tribe member) to a ceremony. He was very kind and very serious. It was immediately obvious to me that this mattered greatly, that he was going to teach me something very important, as I had asked.

He waited until I was ready to go and was sure to tell me repeatedly to learn how to leave as little life force in my body as was necessary for it to function so that the rest of the energy could be used for experiences in the journeys. He was telling me this, not just for today, but teaching me how to release any energy that was holding up my leg or keeping my hand in a position, to find a position that did not require that effort so that the life force could go with me and therefore expand what was possible for me to learn.

When I had done my best, he took me to this place of celebration and had me tune into my senses, what time of day it was, what the ground felt like. It took several tries to orient myself to this place. It was sunrise with a big, traditional circle with a fire in the center and stones demarcating the ceremony area. The ground was a clay-like dirt. He then guided me to watch the ceremony taking place while he explained it to me.

> **We breathe the air. We drink the water. It is in us and we are in it. Our cells long for the fire of the sun and drink it in for life. And every step we take is oneness with the mother earth.**

What he said was that this was a morning ritual, a morning celebration for the awakening. It is true at every level, from the awakening of the day to the awakening of the soul. The ceremony is a joining with the elements of the earth – air, water, earth, and fire. Knowing we are not separate from them but one with them. It is not a ceremony to honor them or thank them but to join with them. It is important for us to know that we are them, and they are us.

In joining with them, we see the world differently. When we know we are one with them our perspective completely changes. We do not take from them and on occasion give to them. We are them. Any destruction or dishonoring that we do of them, we do to ourselves. There is no separation.

When we understand that we are the earth, that her dirt runs through our veins, then we will understand life. When we understand that we are the water, we will no longer treat her the same. You do not waste yourself; you do not disregard yourself – not if you are healthy and certainly not without grave consequences.

It is the most amazing feeling to understand that we are one. In that oneness all makes more sense. There is no separation. I don't know how to put it in words how good it feels to feel that oneness. It is bliss. There are no worries. Nothing matters; there are no worries or concerns. We breathe the air. We drink the water. It is in us and we are in it. Our cells long for the fire of the sun and drink it in for life. And every step we take is oneness with the mother earth. There could be nothing more fundamental.

Begin there. Start there. Breathe in your mother, your ancestor, yourself. Everything that is within her is within you. There can be no other way. In seeing and acknowledging this truth, you come back into alignment with what is. This is truth.

Jeannie Bertoli

This is life. Begin here.
Blessings to you all.

ARE YOU READY TO FACE YOUR EXCUSES?

Good morning. We know you are struggling this morning with your sweet doggie being unwell. We are here today to comfort you and lift you up. You may do the best you can for her, and of course you are, and then you must let the rest be what it will. You know of course that you will see her through her last days, but you do not know that these are those. She has an injury that may well be healed relatively soon. Spend the next days, until you know, caring well for her by making her as comfortable as possible and letting her lie in the sun for its healing properties as well as her enjoyment. Then you will see soon enough; you will know and will proceed from there. Again remember that this may be an injury that is resolvable and resolved. We give you a hug today and encourage you to perk up and give her medicine and let her rest. Do not hover over her; this will not help. And do not make yourself miserable; that will not help.

Okay love. Now on to other matters, as we say, but with particular compassion today as we know you have been in such pain. Let us move on, together.

Today we want to talk to you all about cleanliness and purity. We talk about this in the sense of having a clear understanding of life, clearing away all the junk that makes your understanding of life clouded. Your lives have become so full – full of activity and full of stimuli that it is difficult to carve out a moment for deeper matters. All of the activity in your lives does not necessarily (or usually) add to the overall value or experience of your life...yet it becomes habitualized and engrained, and then remains.

> *All of the activity in your lives does not necessarily (or usually) add to the overall value or experience of your life...yet it becomes habitualized and engrained, and then remains.*

Technology is a prime example. What a wonderful thing it is to be able to have cell phones and not have to stay home to await a phone call. And yet the convenience is overtaken by the immediacy, the primacy that this device demands if you are not careful. Most people attend more to their phones than the experiences in their environment, so they may as well be home with their phone. They are neither engaging with other people, nor with the sun and the wind.

Be cautious to think about what you want your life to be, where you find value, and be sure that your time reflects this. With all the choices available to you all today, it is easy to become over-burdened by over-choosing, and then get lost in the amount of activity you have created for yourselves. This can be true whether you are single or married with children. You can run yourself ragged and have a chaotic life, no matter the logistical circumstances of your life.

Luckily, you can also have a relatively slow, intentional, and peaceful life, no matter your logistics.

Many of you will make excuses why you need to keep this or that circumstance in your life, but it is not true; it is never true. Your choices, your trade-offs are yours and yours alone and reflect your own expanded or limited thinking. This is a harsh reality, meaning a stark reality, and is true for all of you, but few of you will ever truly face this and take this level of responsibility.

No excuse about your choices or behavior is ever, ever true. If you face this, freedom, peace, and health are on the other side. But first you must face what you have done and correct it, clear the plate and begin again.

EXERCISE:

Ask yourself:

- *What if you had no job, no house, no routines, no obligations, nothing...what would you select to go on your plate?*
- *If you find yourself thinking about why what you have is what you 'have to' have, you are back in excuses.*
- *There are no 'have to's,' period. "I can't ____ because of ____" is the most common phrase regarding these matters. It is never, ever true.*
- *Take that look in the mirror and see where you are making excuses.*

We know most of you will reject this exercise because it requires such a level of responsibility and action, but some of you are ready. Some of you are sick of your own excuses, sick of not feeling quite right, sick of knowing something is missing.

This rings true with you, JB, that you have bound yourself with these ways of thinking and have lost much along the way, in the search for some type of false security. On the other side is freedom and expansion, and everything that is possible in this life while you are here.

For those of you, you pioneers, you seekers, we call out to you. Find your way. Call out and we will always be there. Come; clear a path so we may find you again. Clear a path for us so we may begin.

Blessings to all.

RELEASE YOUR GRIP ON WHAT IS
& ALLOW FOR WHAT MAY BE

Good morning. It is a glorious day today. The sun is shining, the birds are beginning to chirp and all is possible. You have before you, each of you, unlimited possibilities, a future that may be only bright. For you, JB, you are getting ready to move; you are preparing yourself and inviting the opportunity for a new home. What an exciting time. It is wonderful to be in the anticipation with you, having no answers and nothing determined. It is so exciting to see what will happen next. Be looking out for signs and inviting the wondrous opportunities that will come. You will find a home in your next place. You will be happy with the climate and the people and the energy. You will find fun there and be happy. You will find true friendships with joyful people. We are happy for you and look forward to your journey into the unknown.

For all of you, too, life is or can be a journey into the unknown and the unending possibilities. What do you wish to grasp? What 'security' are you willing to relinquish? You cannot grab what is new until you release what you are currently gripping. A full plate cannot accommodate more opportunities.

How exciting to think about it. What space will you provide? What opening will you create? Where will you allow for the new?

> ***You have before you, each of you, unlimited possibilities, a future that may be only bright.***

When you create an opening, you will see opportunities fly in. We await your partnership in this. As long as there is a 'no vacancy' sign outside of your house, we have no place to interject. This is not only true in terms of actions but in terms of thoughts. It is true on every level, like fractals. When you have pre-decided upon limits and have filled yourself to those limits, there is not room for anything new.

So many of you state a longing for something new or something different. Be cognizant on every level where you have made room for that new thing. What security have you let go of to open your hand to receive something new?

So many of you want to give up nothing, to not stretch yourself at all, and still to receive. It cannot be this way. You are currently closed off, and in that, there is no opening for us to show up. Yes, there are a few examples of people winning the lottery or some such thing, but two points about that. One, they were open and making efforts and wanting, and two, being the recipient of a windfall is not always the shift that people hope for.

So in your cases, dear ones, we ask you to think about stretching yourselves, thereby realizing how entrenched you are – how you say you want different, better, more, but without work on your behalf – internal, emotional shifting.

Too many want to cling to the old and also receive the new. This is not how it works. What are you willing to give up? How are you willing to shift? What beliefs/issues would you have to face to create the opening to be in relationship with us differently? While the answers are not complicated, they do require a maturity and focus beyond just wishing and hoping.

This new process is the true meaning of the law of attraction – to be in a place of opening to what is possible, to be in touch with the expansion of the universe rather than the contraction.

When you have decided upon something and are clinging to it, like a sense of security, you are in a state of contraction. Imagine your shoulders rounded and your arms pulled into your chest with your hands closed, and your head down. This is a perfect representation of contraction. From this state, there is no flow of life, no living in what is possible.

When you are in a state of expansion, it is like your head is up, your arms are out wide, your chest is up and open, and your hands are open. You are in a state of receptivity, yes, but also in participation in creation – not just for your own benefit but for the benefit of all.

We invite you today to see where in your life you are in a state of contraction and where you are in expansion. For, of course, you are not only one or the other, but both, in different parts of your life.

We invite you this day to be honest with yourself, without blinders, to see where you are helping yourself live the life of your dreams, and where you are getting in your own way. We will always be here to help you get what you want, but know that you are always choosing what you want through these decisions.

We always honor your choice and support you. We will always be with you. Amen.

> *You cannot grab what is new until you release what you are currently gripping. A full plate cannot accommodate more opportunities.*

Jeannie Bertoli

FACING OUR INCONSISTENCIES... FINDING PEACE

Good morning. Today is a good day. What is important for you today is not to try to push or grasp, but to be open, observant, and in the wonder of creation. You will go look at that city as a possible place to live. Stay in the question. Feel the air, feel the energy. Await the opening, the opportunity you seek. Look for signs. Be in excited anticipation rather than clinging and wanting. We know you are ready to leave. We know. It will happen very soon. Listen to the air. See what she tells you. Be in communion with all...and see what happens.

This is true for all of you. You get ideas and goals and agendas, and you go for them or you don't. You go for them based on ideas in your head, or you don't because of emotional and psychological blocks. But we are here to offer you a new way to live – not based on 'you' as such a dominant figure. Instead of being myopically focused on what is going on inside your own processes, listen to the wind...align yourself with the earth.

You are not alone in this world, and there are not just people on this earth. There is so, so, so much more. The energy of all living things is alive and well. The energies of those from other worlds are here, too. You know this in your core.

You have senses beyond how you were raised, beyond those of the brain, touch, sight, smell, etc.

Most of you are not taught and do not think holistically, and on every level (like the study of fractals). What is done on the cellular level is done on the global level. You cannot be disrespectful to animals and kind to your child. You cannot put poisons in the water and go to church on Sunday and have that work. It does not. You create confusion when you each do not live in a congruous manner.

> *Without an integrated, considered life, you will get no more than what you have.*

You are now blinded. So many live based on some rationalization of them being a good person and doing the best they can. This is an interesting story, but nothing more. Without an integrated, considered life, you will get no more than what you have.

When you wonder why your government does not have consistency, you need look no further than your own life. That is why. You speak of love but attack and kill others throughout the world. You speak of a demand for ethical behavior towards you and you hire torturers and then justify it. You selfishly invade other lands due to 'your' interests. But there is no 'your'; it is 'our'...our interests.

What is good for the water and good for the people is good for the countries and the world entire. There is no separation. There is no one or the other. When companies care only about shareholders to the dismissal of their employees or their customers, this will not work. It creates a fracture.

This is no different than how you live your lives. You justify treating some people well and others not well because you judge some as good, others as guilty, some worthy of pity, and others barely worthy of life. This cannot work. It is an inconsistency in your character.

You cannot be loving, put poison in your body, participate in war or the slaughtering of the animals or the stripping of the earth. They cannot fit together in any neat fashion and everything be alright. These inconsistencies cause fractures.

These concerns only for self shall never prevail. You shall destroy yourselves, destroy others, and destroy the planet.

Think of all the people you don't care about – perhaps those in prison or those from other religions or other countries, or the very rich or the very poor. Who gets your kindness and who gets your judgment, and then who is just dismissed as irrelevant?

The same is true about animals – which do you love, which do you hate, and to which do you turn a blind eye? Do you really think this is the way nature is set up – that some matter and others don't? Does this match with your image of God, loving some and not others? It could never be true.

We could give you many more examples at every level – some insects you treasure, some you hate, and some you dismiss. When you enact these totally fabricated ways of being, you create fractures. These are not currently being healed. You are creating fractures in your health as you create them in the air, the water, the food you intake, and the energy you put out in the world.

To what do you turn a blind-eye? People are made fun of for being 'tree-huggers' when they care about waste and landfills and whales and dolphins. Why is that?

Why is that people who care about themselves, their 'own' people, profits, and consuming – those people are a 'normal' part of a capitalistic society? But those who actually think about these matters in holistic ways and care about everything that is done – they are somehow dismissed or diminished.

Then there is personal behavior – whether wasting food by putting it in trash or using plastic or Styrofoam bags or containers that are then thrown out. We ask you this day to begin thinking about and noticing the myriad ways in which this is how you are living. Again, at every level, this fracturing equates to illness and destruction. Those who have the courage to think about their own behavior, challenge themselves, become consistent in a message of love and joy and peace – these people change the world.

This, by the way, does not mean changing and then picking fights with those still living the 'old' way. It means changing yourself, living in peace and joy and love and compassion, allowing others to see your example, and creating products and services based upon these principles. That is the answer you seek.

You, JB, saw recently a documentary where the head of a company never took compensation that was more than five times that of its lowest paid employees. That is wonderful. Triple bottom line – also wonderful. The justification of stock markets and corporations – not wonderful.

But do not create a fight about it…create an alternative.

Create an alternative. Be in love with all living things.

Dismiss not the rivers or the rocks or the trees or the insects or animals. Love all; respect all.

Let your production not destroy but uplift. We will leave you with that, though we could go on. We hope some of you will have your eyes opened today. This is critically important for you.

Jeannie Bertoli

> ***Those who have the courage to think about their own behavior, challenge themselves, become consistent in a message of love and joy and peace – these people change the world.***

YOU ARE LOVED

Good morning. We are glad you are here with us this day. We are really surprised you are here today given all that has occurred. Last night was your last shift at the hospital, you gave notice at your house, got to bed at one in the morning, and still you are here. We honor your devotion to this service.

Also, you have been very supported lately by strangers, acquaintances, friends, and professionals. We pause to acknowledge them as well. We honor their contributions to your life. We also know you need some physical affection from a man and that will be coming to you very shortly. Companionship and connection is on the way in your new home.

Now on to other matters. We are going to speak briefly and simply today. You are loved. All of you are so incredibly loved beyond your wildest imaginations. Whatever your ideas of great love are, you are loved at least 100 exponents beyond that. You are surrounded at all times by loving energy that wants nothing more than to love and support you.

We encourage you to take the time to tune into this Source. It surrounds you at all times, in all situations. Feel into it, knowing it is there. Yes, you may sense other feelings or energies first, but look for it, seek it. Behind the blocks it is always there.

We have spoken and will speak many more times about removing those blocks, but that is not for today.

Today we simply want you to feel some measure of how loved you are. Sense it today.

Blessings to you all.

> *Today we simply want you to feel some measure of how loved you are.*

Jeannie Bertoli

HEALTH & ILLNESS
(PART ONE)

Good morning dear one. We are glad you are with us this Saturday morning. Know that you do not have to do this every day and do not feel pressured to do so now that you are publishing them. Remain in a place of savoring the experience. You love this time and this communication so much. Do nothing to yourself that would take away from that. Worry not how people will take what is said. That is not yours to worry about. Be in peace, child.

Now on with the day. So today we want to talk to you about health and illness and how each is a process. As your back was hurting this week, you began to get this lesson and even said it out loud. When each of you describes wellness and illness, you describe a symptom – "I'm feeling great today" or "My back is hurting today." How you got there is a matter of each choice and alignment with the processes of life (explained below).

Let us take your back as an example. You are a runner. You run about five times per week. You long ago stopped all stretching and probably haven't done so in eight months. You were doing other practices that were stopping you from having any noticeable symptoms of that. But each time you did not stretch, your muscles contracted and became the tiniest bit less flexible. These are your muscles throughout your legs, including around your knees, all the muscles around your behind and lower back. The 'illness' wasn't the symptom of a painful back – the real illness was the process of not taking care of your body as it needed for it to stay well.

> ***You align your life with health or you align with illness.***

So we are asking you today to re-think wellness, and illness. Think of the everyday alignment. You align your life with health or you align with illness. You either eat well or you don't. You make these choices throughout each day. So too, you make choices toward mental health that include a focus on gratitude, compassion, and peace…or not.

If you simply have your normal reactions, you may find yourself focusing on the frustrations of the world and how situations did not go as you wished. You choose health or illness with every part of you.

The body, the form, is susceptible to what you 'feed' it, meaning what you take in. Your thoughts are influenced by your growing-up environment and the media you take in and the people with whom you spend time. Your bodies crave the sugar and salt and fat of processed foods if you take them in. Your body and mind crave more of what you feed it. Know this when you defend how you feel and the things you desire. Notice your reactions. Become aware of the music and television that you prefer. This tells you something about you and where you are today.

You can always change your thought and feeling patterns, but this is great insight as to where you are today.

Jeannie Bertoli

HEALTH & ILLNESS
(PART 2)

To pick up on yesterday's message, you can retrain your mind to think in terms of alignment and how you want to live your life rather than symptoms and symptom abatement. What do you believe are the choices that align with illness? With wellness?

We will get you started. Firstly, know that all systems flow together, so physical illness/wellness is of course completely tied to emotional, psychological, and spiritual illness/wellness. So if your thinking and actions align with competitiveness and anger, you are in the flow of illness. Enough anger, enough suppression, and cancer, heart attack, or some other medical symptom can easily occur.

Too many of you will see this and immediately think it does not refer to you, but look more deeply. Where does your heart have bitterness? Where are you holding onto the wrongs of others? Where do you react with defensiveness or rationalization? These are the places where there is not purity, not an alignment with wellness. This is a message for all of you.

The people who are religious and attend church on Sundays – how many of them do you know that are so kind while there but within a few hours (or a few minutes) are driving offensively, snapping at their spouses, or in other ways at one with frustration or bitterness.

It is time to let go of your burdens – yes, your burdens. When you carry around anger or bitterness toward another person or just in life, it is your burden. It is time to lay such things down. Release yourself. Come back to a place of pure intent. Allow others to have their issues and be themselves without taking that on yourself and creating such illness in your own life. Your perspective, your mood, your energy is your responsibility. Lay down these burdens for yourself, and without judgment of others.

> ***It is this journey to wellness that offers you the lessons of this lifetime.***

Please generalize from what was said here to the appropriate terms for your life. Do not get into semantics and see where this does not fit you. Change the words a bit and see where it does. It fits for all of you, we promise. See where you are not in purity of intent and begin those releases. Ask yourself what it would take to be aligned with wellness in those areas where you are not.

Notice any excuses or rationalizations you make for why this is not realistic or not applicable. We promise, it is both realistic and applicable. It is this journey to wellness that offers you the lessons of this lifetime.

Be in peace and listen. We love you all very much.

Jeannie Bertoli

WHAT ARE YOU NUMBING?

Good morning. We are glad you are here with us today. We remind you to be gentle with yourself. The experiences and transitions that keep occurring for you lately are so new and have not yet settled in your mind and body. You are doing so well, though, and are following our guidance. We bow to you for your steadfastness with this. This is the freedom of life. It is the answer that you long sought and most others seek through other means.

At first, you attempted to find this place within by trying to attract the right people and circumstances into your life to make you feel good, happy, and peaceful. Other people have also sought these feelings in many ways, from positive thinking to different forms of escapism, to just accepting their life, feeling sad but resigned to it.

You have seen, and we tell you again now, that these methods are not effective. There are other answers that will bring you into deep peace and joy. Life is not about putting up with a bunch of difficult and sad situations. Life is not about escaping from those things, or from life itself.

If you feel better about life or enjoy it more when you are wasted, what does that say about life? If you need to alter your mood to be relieved or peaceful, what does that say about the default mood from which you are escaping? Why does letting loose not occur in everyday life? What are you loosening through these means?

From what prison do you free yourself? Think about it.

If you think about how much of your time is spent managing how you feel, you may be surprised! Drinking, smoking, prescription and street drugs, television, food, shopping, gambling, sex, and even exercise are often used to alter your state of mind.

> *If you feel better about life or enjoy it more when you are wasted, what does that say about life?*

So, the first few questions are: What are you altering from? What are you escaping from? What are you feeling?

Slow down and answer that. What are you feeling? There is something going on that you wish to numb out and escape from, or that causes you to feel anxious or sad. What is it? What has you stressed to the point that you reach for ____ (fill in the blank)?

For many of you, the first layer of the answer may be busyness, that you are stressed by the volume of activity in your life. There are many layers of the answer to go through to get to peace. These layers are habits, teachings, and wounds that cover over each other. Often, they were originally solutions you implemented to solve unease at a lower layer, but then became a problem as you did it to excess or it just became another layer of numbing that stopped working. When it stopped working, you kept it and covered it with yet another layer that may have worked for a time.

Many people smoke marijuana or drink alcohol most days to alter their experience of life. What is happening in your life for altered reality to feel better than unaltered reality? Few seem to be looking at the bigger picture, that their regular life isn't the high, and perhaps that is a problem to face rather than escape from.

There is nothing inherently wrong with drinking or taking drugs to alter your mood. But think about what is happening in your life that causes you to feel so much better with that drug in your system. Remember, this drug can be buying shoes, eating mood-altering food, gossiping about other people, gambling, etc. You must look at your own life and see what you do to alter.

This partial list is not offered for you to point your finger at others, but for you to find yours if it is not listed. Perhaps it is pleasing others or drama in some form. Keep searching yourself. Keep the emphasis on your journey within. Most people use something habitually.

Again, there is nothing wrong with using these means with some moderation, but we would suggest that you notice what you are doing and seek an effective way to heal why you are doing it. Get to a place of dealing with your wounds and habits and why the life you are living is not working for you.

You have been taught many ways to live that do not work well. Families and societies simply pass on the systems to you. It is now up to you to realize that the methods do not serve you. That is the cry of your feelings. They are screaming, "This is not working for me! Pay attention!"

Will you? We hope so.

That is all for today.

Blessings to you all.

> *You have been taught many ways to live that do not work well. Families and societies simply pass on the systems to you. It is now up to you to realize that the methods do not serve you.*

THE BIGGEST DECISION – RELEASING THE DISTRACTIONS OF EARTHLY LIFE

Good morning. We are glad you are with us today. There is so much to be learned, so much more to which you may be exposed. You have begun the journey and are attending to the most important aspects by disengaging yourself from the beliefs that once limited you so greatly. As long as you believe the external world is what is real and focuses your time and energy on manipulating that world to make yourself comfortable, you are limited to that focus and belief system.

Once you come to realize that the earthly realm is only a projection of your mind and a stage on which you play out the reasons for your lifetime, you free yourself for all that is to come. When you understand that you are a part of the Universe, including universal wisdom, the matters of the earth are petty in comparison. They are still important, though, and you must remain invested enough to care about life on earth and to use the ways and things of the earth to their purpose. But remaining somewhat invested in earthly matters is not hard.

Most people, as you know, become overly involved and invested in the matters of the earth, and live from that place. It is so easy to fill your minds with the stimuli around you; then that occupation creates a self-sustaining life.

Your thoughts are filled with the people and events around you as well as devices used for distraction and entertainment (television, computers and the Internet, phones, and video games). As long as these are your focuses and where you give your energy, that is all you will get out of life. The extent to which you stay earthbound, you will reap only earthbound bounties from this life. Inversely, the extent to which you broaden your perspective and your focus on spiritual matters, the more your joy and bounty will be from both realms.

> ***When you understand that you are a part of the Universe, the matters of the earth are petty in comparison.***

So many are stuck right at that choice. Earthly life is so consuming and having been entrenched in its ways for so long, releasing this hold is the one of the biggest and most difficult decisions on your journey.

You needn't make this change in a way that makes you uncomfortable. It is not a matter of leaving the known for the unknown. It doesn't need to be done all at once or precipitously. You may build trust over time with the forces of the universe, gaining comfort that they will support you well beyond the limits of this lifetime. Opening yourself to these concepts and developing relationships in other realms are the beginning steps. You can begin today by sitting in silence, declaring your openness, and listening for what comes.

As you invest in life as it can be, you will feel less tied to life as it is. The deep peace and freedom experienced as a result will entice you the rest of the way, for there is nothing on earth that feels as good as universal peace, community, and love.

That is all for today.

Blessings to you all.

> *The extent to which you broaden your perspective and your focus on spiritual matters, the more your joy and bounty will be from both realms.*

WHAT WE BEAM OUT TO THE WORLD

Good morning. We are glad you are here today dear one. Today we will talk to you about vibrations. Right now you are tingling from the journeying/drumming you were just doing. We are shifting a vibrational force for you and will talk to you about those forces now.

It is vibrations that determine, like a radio wave, what you send out and therefore what comes back to you. This is true about the people and circumstances you draw into your life. It is all sourced from you and the vibrations you put out. Since what determines which vibrations you send out is very complicated, we will address that in pieces over time. For today, we want to introduce you to vibrations.

The neurotransmitters in your brain, your belief systems, your wounds, and many other factors go into what vibrations you send out. You are always sending out vibrations like electromagnetic fields. If you are very still, you can experience it. We just gave you, JB, the experience of it.

JB: It feels to me like what it would be like to be in the middle of an electric current.

That is a good analogy. You are the center of the course, like the nucleus of that atom. You are both the sender of the beam and within each beam/current/vibration. These words are used here interchangeably. You are the sender and within every element of each message. And the world is a large mirror, so at some point your beam 'hits' something/someone and is bounced back to you. The person/situation that shows up isn't so much 'real' (as it is currently treated) as it is you coming back to you, just a reflection of yourself.

> ***The stimuli you attend to are the ones that are beaming you back to yourself, are a reflection of the vibrational force you beam out every micro-second.***

Now we realize that this can be very difficult for you all to take in because you get so many people and situations that show up in your life that cause you discomfort or worse. And it would be very difficult for you to believe you drew those in, that they were just a reflection of you. Part of the difficulty there is in not understanding all the factors that go into what you are beaming out.

There are two main points we will make about this today. Firstly, we want to say that many, many people and situations come into your life, come across your path, and only some of them do you attend to, positively or negatively. That is one indicator to you of what you are beaming out. You only attend to certain people and situations – the ones that trigger you. These triggering people and situations are there for you. We have discussed in other places how you may interact with these people and situations to understand why they are there, to extract from them their value.

Briefly, they are here to teach you or to show you and help you heal your wounds. These wounds may be from previous lifetimes, childhood in this lifetime, or even yesterday. They may remind you that you are imbalanced in some way or not living according to your values, for example. Each similar occurrence of a trigger is an opportunity for you to resolve that wound. You need not, and if you do not, you will have another opportunity with the next, similar trigger.

So the first thing we want you to recognize is that of all the billions of stimuli constantly occurring around you, you attend to only a few thousand. Therefore, by deduction, you can see that you have an element of choice in your experience. Then we are telling you that the stimuli you attend to are the ones that are beaming you back to yourself, are a reflection of the vibrational force you beam out every micro-second. You also notice what matches your existing belief systems, so one person may experience an event with gratitude and another person may experience that same event with suspiciousness. There is always more than you experience...much, much more. The great news about this is that there is always love available, always beauty, wonder, and joy. You may select them at any time.

In our second point today, we want you to have a basic understanding of what you are beaming out and why. You come to this life with previous wounds and skills, goals/lessons for this life, connections with other souls, and of course, a connection to God/Oneness/The Universe. That is a good list to start with. So in other words, you come to this life with karma (wounds and skills, good and bad – in your words), soul groups, lessons for this lifetime, a deeper knowing of All That Is, and a connection to all life.

Given all of that, Life is a vibrational force, so you are beaming out those things listed above. You are beaming your existence, your story to the world in every moment.

People select clothes or cars or degrees or attitudes to put on and represent themselves to the outer world. Think of this as a different version of that, an inherent and un-erring one. You are, and so while you are in this form in this place, you beam out who you are...constantly. Try to absorb that. We know it is big, very different from how you were raised and a different way to think about life.

One of the outcomes of this is that when people 'know' things they have no logical reason to know, they may be paying attention to these vibrations and listening to that information. And we will throw in one other twist, you need not be around someone to 'read' their beam. You can bring them into your consciousness and sense them...

That is all for today. We thank you for going this deeply with us. We are excited for those who will take this material in.

Blessings to you all.

> **The great news about this is that there is always love available, always beauty, wonder, and joy. You may select them at any time.**

"A BEAUTIFUL DETACHMENT"

Good morning. You have had a morning of what you would call 'good news' and 'bad news'. This is a wonderful time to point out that this is the way life goes. It is critical that you understand that things that please and displease you will come around, those that make your life easier and harder, those that move you forward or hold you back. This is the way of it. This is actually good news but we are not going to talk to you about that piece today.

Today is about understanding this process, that this is the way life is, full of situations you prefer and those you do not prefer. Given that, you have a direct choice for peace or anxiety/displeasure. The way of peace comes in knowing that this is the way of it and not 'hoping' for the good and 'dreading' the bad. When you know that each day will have both, peace comes in not attaching to either set of events.

You begin to look at it from a different perspective. Instead of dreading one and anticipating another, they can both become neutral events that do not cause a reaction. Instead you can begin to feel into them and examine them totally differently. As you observe each with what we call 'a beautiful detachment', you can wonder what each is here to teach you, why it has shown up in your life.

As you ask these or similar questions, you have a different relationship with the events of your life. You see them from a different vantage point, really a different dimension, because with this shift you see life differently. You cease to be in the world in the same way. You are somewhat removed from it, and in so doing, you see with a larger perspective and the

> ***This single lesson, this single shift would completely change your life. Can you see it? Can you sense it?***

objectivity of the observer. Of course you are not totally objective, but removed enough to not be clinging to 'good' and running from 'bad' and not seeing that each is there for far bigger reasons than your reactivity.

Can you imagine not attaching to some events as good and others as bad? Imagine the emotional energy you would reserve toward focus and progression on other goals.

Thank you for listening.

Blessings to you all.

Jeannie Bertoli

THE POWER OF FEAR IN EVERYDAY LIFE

Good morning. Today is a great day for you. You will accomplish much, or we should say much will come together. You work very hard, stay focused and on-task. Today you will see how some of that has worked out for you. Things will come back to you that you did not expect. Someone will reach out to you today or reach back on something you had initiated. It will be an affirmation. We are telling you this so that you will know that we know and have another piece of the puzzle as to how life works.

You want to know how life works. You want to know how your friend who did a healing practice on you the other day could see 50 people/entities show up to support you, and how that could play out in your earthly life.

Before we get into that, we also want to say it is really great how you integrate information like that to make it 'normal' or 'regular' in your mind and therefore in the minds of many others. For you there is now a seamlessness between being very, very earthly and grounded in the matters occurring there, and spiritual experiences with beings that are not visible or audible in a typical way. As you have come this far down the path, it has become so integrated, not just in your experience, but also in your mind, that it feels completely normal. It is just another part that makes the whole. As such, you will represent that well and make the world a better place as a representative of light.

We are very happy for you, and for that. Happy for you in that the more you take in light and truly incorporate it in your life (in a very basic, chemical way), the more deeply happy and peaceful you will be. You will fear nothing, as you will know there literally is nothing to fear. You will take more risks, live

> **When you truly know that there is nothing to fear, life dramatically changes.**

more adventurously, live more and more closely aligned with your true nature, which is very fun and adventurous. When you truly know that there is nothing to fear, life dramatically changes. And of course this is true for all of you. When you truly know there is nothing to fear, life changes. What would happen if you did not worry about/fear financial matters? What if you did not fear a relationship ending or a job ending or a move or the rejection of others?

You have been soooo indoctrinated into fear to a degree almost no one recognizes: fear if you don't finish school, get the right job, stay in that town, get that mortgage, etc. On and on we could go. Wear your seatbelt or else something terrible could happen. Wear that helmet or else something terrible could happen. Get home before dark or something terrible could happen. The list goes on and on.

Parents indoctrinate fear into their children based on the tragedies of a few. In absolute terror that these 'tragedies' could happen to you, widespread laws, regulations, and policies are enacted which restrict the many who would never have been touched.

But this is not actually the problem. The unseen and unrecognized problem is that fear has been instilled. And when the thinking process becomes about fear and tragedy prevention, the process can no longer be about embracing fear and risk taking. It cannot be about the adventure when it is about 'don't' and 'no'.

This is a very deep message that most will dismiss but is nonetheless very valuable. It is very difficult to be in the fear and worry, and also be in the wonder and adventure.

The two do not easily co-exist.

It takes a brave soul at this time to examine the degree to which you are living in fear and have made fear a part of your decision-making process on all levels. How much of your life is significantly determined by fear? How much are you teaching that process to the next generation? How much is 'be careful' emphasized vs. how much 'be adventurous', 'live boldly', and 'seize life' are?

This is incredibly powerful and life-altering, should you allow it to be. To how many people have you recommended the book The 4-Hour Workweek by Timothy Ferris – which is a step-by-step manual for financial freedom – not a quick fix, but a genuine how-to manual? How many people find a way to reject it without fully reading or trying one thing in it?

Fear is deeply, very-deeply entrenched, such that when solutions to fears are offered, you often find a way not to accept them.

We will leave you with that.

To JB: We will address more of the 'how life works' things later. We got off on a tangent.

> *It is very difficult to be in the fear and worry, and also be in the wonder and adventure.*

LOOK BEHIND THE CURTAIN

Good morning. We are excited you are with us today. Your life, your people, are at an exciting point in your history. This is a time of opportunity. It is a time of change. Finally, many forces of darkness no longer have dominance and light has a chance to infiltrate and take over and bring you into a new time. This requires an awakening and an awareness on the part of your people. It is happening in increasing numbers. People are realizing that life as they have known it is no longer acceptable, no longer enough. The chaotic life of job, marriage, and children in constant motion is not good enough. It is not enough to be the measure of a life. There is more. There is much more.

And with the realization, the opportunity presents itself. This is how it happened for all those who were awakened, including you. One way or another each of you saw through the illusion, the façade that, like in The Wizard of Oz, only required you to look behind the curtain. Now you have, many of you have, and many more of you are on the precipice of doing so.

It is so exciting for us to see people wake up, rub the sleep out of their eyes, and look around. They see through the illusion and see the choice before them. Then their hearts can re-engage and be central again. You have not known a time in history when this was dominant, but it has been so. An enlightened, awakened time has been and will be so again.

> **Forces of darkness no longer have dominance and light has a chance to infiltrate and take over.**

To get there, the awakening is the beginning. There must be enough people conscious. Where you are right now is that tons and tons of people feel a stirring. They feel a dissatisfaction or a calling for more…they feel the beginnings. It is those people who will be drawn to those already awake and offering a message of the heart given with pure intent. You, JB, are among those people and there are many others.

You see them around, and you will know them by their purity. These people speak of these deeper matters without compulsion, agenda, or force in any way. They offer it, simply. They have no ownership of it. You have been given information and a process by which people may live. You have been given this to pass it on. That is your piece. Others have different ways. Many are seers or readers; many are healers.

When they deliver their service in deep connection with All That Is and with a purity of intent, others will be increasingly drawn to them. You know many who are drawn to this work, but only partially meet the criteria above. Their ability to be of service will be limited by such. The same is true for all of you. The degree to which you come from ego or protectionism or wounded triggering, your work will be limited to an exponent of that.

It is such a vulnerable place for people to get to, to come to spiritual workers (healers, readers, speakers, and counselors). So if these workers do not have that purity, it does more than not be helpful to that person; it pushes them away from this category of work for some time.

As this is not yet socially acceptable, each worker is a representative of the entire field of work, as it will not be later in time. Each 'quack' makes the newly budding field look like 'quackery'. Therefore be cautious and considered.

You who feel drawn to a different way of life, find others who feel the same way. Find someone you think is further down the path and of pure intent. Form small pockets, small communities.

Come together and speak of such matters. Speak from your heart. Find an opening together. Draw the light toward you and feel supported by the Universe. This is how change happens. Blessings be to the change makers, for you will find great joy.

> *Blessings be to the change makers,*
> *for you will find great joy.*

Jeannie Bertoli

COME BACK TO THE NATURAL STATE

Good morning. First we want to acknowledge how hard yesterday was for you. Watching your little doggie in such discomfort and so incapacitated broke your heart. We know this and we were sad for you and with you. Although we know that you know that all that lives will die, that souls' journeys continue, when you lose your little one you will be incredibly sad and mourn her deeply. Now is not the time for that, but there will be a time, without fail. And the pain will be deep. We will be here with you when that day comes. You are never alone. We will raise her up and give her comfort, and she shall be forever with you. But as we say, that day is not now. Enjoy her there in the time you have left. It is not short but also not long the time you have with her. Simply enjoy each day.

This is true of all relationships. All will end, in this moment or the next, or many moons away. Without that knowledge of when you will part, simply enjoy what you have without the assumption of the next moment. Now on to other matters.

Today we want to talk to you about strength and about pruning. You get very self-critical about imperfect moments or decisions. You are so hard on yourself for eating badly or not exercising enough or not pushing yourself hard enough. It takes very little actions far from perfection before you get quite critical of yourself. This is not how we feel about you and not a joyous way to go through life.

Yes, you are imperfect. Yes, you make decisions and take actions that are not aligned with your best and are not in your best interest. Yes, it is all true, but that is okay. That is a part of your journey. You make the 'bad' decisions and then you learn and move on. You only complicate situations with self-criticism. You add more from which you need to heal.

> *You only complicate situations with self-criticism. You add more from which you need to heal.*

The natural way and flow of this is that you take an action, get a result, accept the feedback and decide to repeat or not repeat the original action. It is a simple feedback loop. When you and others add in shame or recrimination, you are adding emotional elements to the natural process, complicating and convoluting it. You do this because in your childhoods many of you corrected your behavior when you were criticized or shamed and so you learned this as a motivator for change. But it is not so in the natural world and it does not add to the natural system.

Take you, JB, with your food issues. You try so hard to be perfect and set that as a standard, that there is no way for you to meet it all or most of the time, and then you feel like a failure and deal with the emotions of that. Instead, there are much simpler answers. For all of you with food issues, the answers are simple when you take the emotions out of it – the emotions of eating and resisting eating.

Simply eat when and only when you are hungry and eat healthy, nutrient-dense, non-processed food. It is as simple as that. To add more to it is to take away from nature and add in emotions into a non-emotional situation. When you can detangle emotions from the situation, you can see this very simple and easy to follow process. That is it.

Detangle emotions from food. Food is not emotional. You just learned somewhere along the way to make it so, and now you all may make a different decision and allow the body to recalibrate. Eat simple, natural foods. Eat when you are hungry and don't when you are not. That is all.

When you add salts and sugars and processing to the food, you manipulate it and complicate the situation. You make food something else…a fix. It triggers different centers of the brain and takes on different functions. You are now taking it away from nature and its natural purpose in your life.

While we elaborated on this point about food, the same can be said about many areas of your lives. It is the same process with exercise, with work, with purchasing and consuming, and with many other things. You have removed these natural parts of life from their natural states, complicated them and had them function differently in your life than is the intention of nature. Much like GMO foods, when you alter the structure or function of nature, you do not know what you will get.

Strip away these alterations. It is time to come back to nature. Things were setup as they were for a reason, including health and balance. When you try to deconstruct and parse out certain pieces and manipulate to get just what you want, you alter the whole system and there is a ripple effect on all areas of that system. People are affected. The environment is affected. We could take many examples, and you know many.

Just some quick examples...take agri-business. To maximize profits, they strip the land. The slaughter industry destroys the environment and tortures animals to maximize efficiency and yield. The fisheries are depleting species from the oceans. Callousness and carelessness are ruling your systems. Lobbying, oil production, etc., etc., etc.

All of the stories are the same – manipulation of nature for the maximization of greed or power, carelessness about the consequences, a myopic view of what matters. And there are and will be consequences for these processes. There must be. You can only so mistreat nature for so long before the consequences will come to bear.

The consequences of your choices are here and have much more to come – diseased bodies, diseased air, diseased water, and scarcity. The only way to correction is to change these processes, strip away the manipulations in the name of greed and power, and turn to the sides of yourself that want to make this a safe and healthy world aligned with natural laws.

Some are doing this, but not enough. Right now money and power, fear and selfishness are still ruling the day. And everyday people are colluders with those in power as they support the industries that are against natural laws. That is the way to change right now. Bigger is not better. Taking is not okay. Grow and eat natural foods. Save rain water. Fight against greed through supporting local businesses.

Consume less. Spend less. Acquire less. Live more. Savor more. Be more.

Amen.

Jeannie Bertoli

> ***Consume less. Spend less. Acquire less.***
> ***Live more. Savor more. Be more.***

LETTING GO

Good morning. We are glad to see you today. Today is your mother's birthday and your friend's birthday. It is a joyous day. We, again, want to say how glad we are that you and your mother are now in a much more mutually loving, accepting, and freer relationship. This does not mean perfection but an open exchange of love and compassion, even when disagreeing. It is wonderful and we are happy for you.

Now onto other things. Today we want to talk to you about friends. You had dreams last night about two very close friends who are no longer in your life. You had deep, deep relationships and connections for long periods of time with these two men, and they are now gone from your life. It was brought to your dreams to teach you that it is okay to let things flow in and flow out. They are out of your life, probably for the rest of your life, and that is okay. There may be times you feel sadness about this or longing for what once was, but what was, is now gone. Life has moved on for each of you, as it should. Amen.

As life progresses, hold onto nothing – not a job, house, or relationship. Life offers you newness – new opportunities, new thoughts, new feelings, new pulls – and so it is with every other person. Things are for a moment in time, and then they may not be the next moment. And while we know this makes many feel very uncomfortable, it makes it no less true.

You must allow for life. As the new comes in and the old often goes out, you must allow for this knowing. This is your journey and each person's journey in their lives. There is little point in trying to stop the river. What will you gain? If you cling rather than releasing, you will create a series of problems as a result – resentments (on their part for being held back and your part for having to hold them back rather than it being their choice), pain, frustration, etc.

> ***It is time to turn within and see your goals for your own lives.***

Freedom comes in allowing the flow of life and fully accepting what comes, and feeling when it's time to let go. Sometimes people are okay with allowance in their own lives but want others not to have a desire to leave them. That is, of course, silly on its face. And many, many others don't even want a flow, a coming and going, in their own lives. They want to obtain things (roles, positions, 'securities') in their lives and then just hold onto them. While this is a natural feeling given that you were raised to seek security and there is an evolutionary desire for such as well, it will not help you on your journey.

Having goals is wonderful. But be careful because you were raised to have an arbitrary list of goals and roles – make lots of money, obtain education and a 'good' job, marry, have children, and buy a house. These goals have been indoctrinated in you since you were little and are not your goals, but others' for you. *It is time to turn within and see your goals for your own lives.*

The problem is not that the goals others set for you are 'bad' in any way, but they are neither 'good'. So many of you have attained most or all of these things just to be disappointed, as they don't hold the promise offered. Many of you have attained all this just to feel busy and stressed at a minimum, and far worse things like disappointment and overall dissatisfaction with life, and now feel stuck.

So now, today, go within and ask the deeper questions. What is my life about? What am I here for? Let your goals and your dreams and your thoughts and your actions and your focus come from these things.

Let all other expectations of yourself or others go. It is a time to come back to yourselves. And know that this is, of course, never selfish or cruel. When you align your life with larger life and the spiritual purpose of your life, you never come to a place of harm.

So do not fear that. Try it and see what comes. We will go now.

That is all for today.

> ***When you align your life with larger Life and the spiritual purpose of your life, you never come to a place of harm.***

Jeannie Bertoli

FOR ALL THOSE WITH A CALLING

Good morning loved one. This morning you were taken on a journey to a room in what some call the upper world to have some time with your 'team'. Your team is the group of souls and entities that are always there on your behalf – always creating, guiding, teaching you on your path. They have always been with you and always will be. It is a team of support and you are never, ever alone...not even close to it.

So this morning your team had two messages for you: one is that you are going to have all you long for in terms of community, close friendships, and family – all these different forms of love and connection. The other is quite a different message.

The second message is that you are being called to something larger. While this might excite you, you are being told with great seriousness and heaviness to keep you grounded. You are being told to realize that this will be a road with many challenges from the outside world. You will be greatly criticized and ostracized. When you become more influential in this way, many will question and accuse you. You will be confronted with questions and presumptions. Many will not like you for your message, and many others for the process by which you get your messages.

Your team is warning you not to get giddy and excited about this shift, while it will hold moments of great excitement. We know you will embrace those who are ready and are listening. You will love when people understand the messages and make way the path for you to speak further. We are only concerned that you are prepared for when things are otherwise...and they will be.

> ***Become very grounded in what you are doing and why you are doing it. Be not swayed by the voices of others or the masses.***

Prepare yourself for negativity, for all change agents must. You have experienced this on a small level in your life so far, but as you gain exposure and influence, so it will be proportionally more, even exponentially so.

Those in your life will support you as they have journeyed with you and understand the process you have been through and your long hesitancy to accept this into your life. It is those exposed to you for the first time, strangers who hear only your message and your claims as to outside sources of guidance and love and support – they will be those hurling criticism and accusations your way.

The good news is that this is not the time of old and you are in no physical danger. Simply be aware and be prepared. As you can, answer hate and anger with peace and understanding. People do not understand what this is; you did not either for a very long time. And you do not know much of it now, only you accept that it is and embrace it for what it offers.

This message applies for all who have a seriousness of purpose. Become very grounded in what you are doing and why you are doing it. Be not swayed by the voices of others or the masses. Know that your purpose is yours alone and denying it would be yours alone. It is your decision. Accepting it and enacting it without peace should be your last option. Do not 'take up your cross' and then complain or feel like a victim. Do your work; fulfill your purpose only if you are prepared to do so with dignity and peace, representing him/Him/those who gave it to you.

JB: This was an unusually serious message this morning. I was surprised, but when it continued as such, I listened closely and took it in.

> ***Fulfill your purpose only if you are prepared to do so with dignity and peace.***

ARE YOU WILLING TO EXAMINE YOUR OWN HEART?

Good morning. We are glad to see you today. It is an interesting day in an interesting time. Yesterday you had such a big day and much will continue to happen as a result. Many steps were taken yesterday that progressed efforts you are making. This is all wonderful. All you must do is stay grounded, stay in your spiritual practice, stay in a place of wonder and non-attachment and all of that will lead to non-reactivity.

You have much going on in the next several days, a very busy schedule to pull logistics together. You need not be hurried or come out of a place of peace. Stay in a place of deep peace and knowing and stay with the flow of life. Do not get rushed and reactive. Stay in a place of an open heart and allowance. This will make the experiences of the next few days vastly different. Feel that difference now? Good. Stay in that place.

We know you are noticing things within the people around you, a lack of congruity, what your profession calls a splitting or lack of solid self. Although this is particularly true where you live, it is true of human nature right now. And it is a good thing.

People are split into different parts – how they are with their friends, how they are with their families, then co-workers and strangers. They are vastly different with those who could be considered 'their people' than those who are 'others'. Others is often split into friendly, non-threatening others, and then all 'other' others.

> ***We are not suggesting that you allow yourself to be 'mistreated'. We are suggesting you look at these situations totally differently.***

People are fine enough to the friendly, non-threatening others, but all 'other' others get a quick tongue and a sharp heart. There is often an immediate defensiveness in people right now, especially at work and very often in customer service jobs. Many of you reading this will notice it in your friends, family, others, and possibly yourself, if you are willing to look.

EXERCISE:
Ask yourself:
- *Who gets your kindness?*
- *Who gets the softness within you?*

- *How is that you justify the difference between this and those who get the worst in you?*
- *Do you blame the 'other'?*
- *Who gets your criticism and sharpness?*
- *Why is that?*

We say this not to judge but so that you may see yourselves more clearly. Being willing and able to take that difficult look at your own ways of being is the first step to changing your life. You must begin to see how far you have come from a path of an open heart, knowing there is no reason for protectionism and defensiveness.

Defenses only work to close your heart. The only real defense in life is knowing no one has the power to hurt you. You do not need to take on the energy of others. When you come across people who offer you disdain, unkindness, or worse, you may breathe it in, and breathe out peace. You need not rise to the occasion to stand with them toe-to-toe.

When you get in a mindset of 'no one is going to treat me that way' then you are coming from a similar place as the instigator. Now there are two angry people, and there is no peace.

These are really tricky situations to change if you have been in a habit of reactivity. We are not suggesting that you allow yourself to be 'mistreated'. We are suggesting you look at these situations totally differently.

When you begin to see the other person as having their own process with their own wounds, then there is no need to react, no need to get involved, let alone drawn in. You may stay on your own path, which hopefully is peace. When you don't see the two of you as connected, then it doesn't say anything about you that this person is just standing there doing what they are doing. You are separate and need not get entangled. That is a huge first step and the most important piece.

For those who would want to take it to another level, you may introduce peace, kindness, and compassion into the situation, all the while knowing that it may be rejected. And if that rejection happens, not to turn that into a place of judgment, but rather you were simply doing your own process and they need not react or respond to it – see the parallel?

When someone is defensive or snappy with you before you even say anything (and so you know you didn't trigger their mood), you may lower the register of your voice and go to an extra kind place as you speak. You may add in more 'please's' and 'thank you's' with a deep sincerity and compassion that may seep through. Of course these are not obligations, but opportunities.

At the beginning, when you first start to feel others' energy, most of you will feel an immediate desire to withdraw from those with harsh energies. That is fine. This is the next step after that, or perhaps several steps down.

The first step, to go back, is about not taking others' energies and actions personally. Staying separate from them helps you not get entangled.

And even before that, the first steps as you choose to go down this path are about facing yourself. This is often the hardest part and so where many people will stop. There are many defenses and rationalizations for being as you are, allowing yourself to go to a place of unkindness and why that is okay. When you start examining these places, it is often very painful. But without this self-examination, no other true progress can be made. It all begins with an examination of your own heart, being willing to take the blinders off.

So many of you convince yourselves you do things from a place of goodness when it really is a place of manipulation or wanting something back, like adulation, acceptance, or respect. Be careful or you will easily fool yourselves. Just because your actions may be kind or self-sacrificing does not mean your intent is good. If you have eyes to see, you will see it. If you are willing to ask the questions, the answers are there.

Begin your journeys, seek your answers…it is the only way to true peace because at the end of the day there is no shortcut, and there is no fooling anyone. The truth is the truth and no one else need know it for it to be true, even you. So if you fool your own consciousness into believing your story, the truth of how and why you do what you do remains.

We are excited for those of you beginning and on the journey to peace. Welcome. We will support you always.

> *It all begins with an examination of your own heart. Be willing to take the blinders off.*

Jeannie Bertoli

ALIGN YOURSELF WITH
THE FLOW OF LIFE

Good morning. We are glad you are here today. Today is another lovely day that will be filled with openings for you. Yesterday was a great day. You stayed in the exploration of the day and had unexpected openings come your way. Today will be the same. And that is the way of it. When you are in the surrender of life and in the wonder of it, life shows up for you in beautiful and unexpected ways.

We do not mean that each day will be filled with excitement or wonderful, new opportunities, but in a sense, it can always be like that. When you are in joy experiencing your dog, wonder is there. When you are in joy listening to some new information about a subject that interests you, wonder is there. Especially if you can stay away from judging an experience as good or bad, and stay away from getting triggered by it, wonder is there.

Another piece of this, also, is that not every day brings the expansion of new opportunities. You, JB, are in a time in life and a time in your life where the flow is toward expansion and opening. This is cyclical. Last year you had most of the year in contraction. You had an ending of an important relationship, a move to a place where you knew no one, and a period where you were called to spend much time alone in study, information gathering, and contemplation.

Knowing that there are these cycles helps all of you to not attach to what 'should' be. If you are listening, not with your ears, you will feel the difference quite easily. And the more you can align your vibration with the vibration of life, the easier and more peaceful life will be.

So when you have your goals and your agendas that are coming from your own aspirations, along with cognitive and emotional desires, they may not be aligned with the flow of life. When this is the case, you will find progression toward and achievement of your goals more difficult.

> *Life can be as simple as these factors – stay in purity of intent, and listen and align yourself with the flow of life.*

There can be extraordinary effort required to get to the same place that another time would have been little effort. This is the point we make to you today. You may fight the flow of life; that is certainly your choice. But the more you align yourself, the more you will see 'life' show up for you. Doors open; opportunities literally present themselves before you.

You will see consistent openings and synchronicities when two things are in place: you are in purity of intent and you are aligning yourself with the flow of life. This is the place of the deepest joy and peace. You will notice that we slipped in the 'purity of intent' piece as a reminder of the importance of that factor. Life can be as simple as these factors – stay in purity of intent, and listen and align yourself with the flow of life.

Now you may never do those things 100% and there is a journey to get to on these paths, but this is still the bottom line. To get to purity of intent is a journey. To learn to come out of your head and your triggers and listen to and become aligned with life, that too is a journey.

When you do those things consistently and increasingly, you will see dramatic changes in your life. How you make the switch to that kind of life…well, that is a dramatic shift from the current way life is led. It is a journey away from the foci taught by your society and one aligned with the natural laws. The only question is: are you ready to make that dramatic change?

Blessings to you all this day.

Jeannie Bertoli

MAKE THE MOST OF YOUR TIME HERE

Good morning. Hello love. We know you are not feeling great today and we want to acknowledge that before we go on to say how excited we are. This is an amazing time of manifestation for you and many others. The speed of progress is wonderful for us to watch. Many of you are focused, in communion with life, and racing toward a new life. How wonderful!

For those who wish to be more on this path, we say find someone whom you sense is doing it. Ask them about it. Wonder how you can get there too. It is a shift in focus, a change in the way you live your life. It is a time where, if truly searching, you will find similar souls seeking to make the change. Find each other and find a leader/mentor/coach to help you. They are recognizable, if you have eyes to see. They are grounded and peaceful and with great joy. They have a laser-like focus and are not interested in the pettiness so prevalent around you.

Create small groups of purpose. And do much each day to make the shift. It requires mostly a focus and a desire. With the desire you will make a plan of action, and with a focus you will enact it. Be prepared that much will change as you change. Just by changing yourself, others will feel challenged. Your interests will shift and so will many relationships.

This comes with any major change, and it will with this as well. If you are more concerned with trying to maintain your life as it is today than embracing the path of change and wherever it leads you, you may not want to make this shift. This is not a thing of silliness and cannot be done with one toe and not the rest of your body. This is not a game, as you will quickly find out.

> *For those of you who are ready and willing, and there are many, great peace and joy await you on the other side. No fear, no obstacles can own you after you transition.*

You know those people who say they want to lose weight but are not willing to make a plan for their new food choices or exercise regime – it is the same here. If you are not willing to do what it takes to make the change, no change will occur. No need for pretense; it will not happen. For those of you who are ready and willing, and there are many, great peace and joy await you on the other side. No fear, no obstacles can own you after you transition. No earthly matter is of concern, for you see matters here for what they are – stages set for your learning and healing. All of them are here for that. All of them.

All the places where you think of having bad luck or bad circumstances, including terrible things that occur in childhood and create deep wounds, all are there to serve you for your learning. You will not understand this fully, perhaps, but if you begin down this path, you will realize or come to sense that all is there to serve you. You have wounds from past lifetimes to heal.

You have lessons to learn from past experiences (karma) that these experiences serve. Remember that you are always learning and trying to heal. That is what these experiences are helping you do. In addition, there are those among you who want to be an example of love in the world and serve the world by offering it light with pure intent.

Those people, too, have wounds to heal and lessons to learn. They will be incorporated together. Almost nothing is binary – you are wounded or not, a source of light or not. Healers are wounded, and the wounded are healers. You are all, all of it. You have the full potential of every characteristic within you at each moment.

But some of you are more focused on drama and the stories of earthly life. And some of you are more focused on a deeper connection and knowing, challenging yourself to making the most of your time there. You may do either without our judgment. It is your life and your choice. If you do not focus on these matters now, you will do so in the future.

Blessings to you this day.

> *In addition, there are those among you who want to be an example of love in the world and serve the world by offering it light with pure intent.*

HELPING PEOPLE TRANSITION & NOT OFFER A HOME FOR PAIN

You can be of great assistance to each other during times of transition. In fact, transitions are an important part of every life and happen throughout all lives. In the natural flow of life, there is an approach and a going away, a flow in and a flow out. When relationships, jobs, or anything else leave our lives, or even enter our lives, this is a transition. We more usually recognize the leaving as the difficult transition.

People die, loved ones die, we die. In our culture, we do not see or incorporate this as one of many, many transitions within a life and within the larger life. For within the larger life, there are many lifetimes and many deaths. And then within each of those are many 'mini-deaths' as well, which are simply transitions.

We transition when we move, graduate, change jobs, etc. But we also transition when we take on a new habit, a new way of thinking, etc. And we often are letting go of one thing as we acquire another.

There is an opportunity here to help people understand the role of transition in their lives, to learn a series of questions or a process by which we may help each other. By learning this process, we may be of service during the very small transitions but also during times of larger transition. Instead of offering the normal 'comfort' during these times, we may offer real assistance.

> *The more we simply make a comfortable space for pain, the more it will unpack and make a home.*

EXERCISE: Some questions we might ask are:
- *Are you ready/prepared for this transition?*
- *What would you need to be prepared?*
- *Is this transition in your best interest?*
- *How would you know if this were the right time for this transition?*
- *What does your highest guidance tell you about this?*
- *How may I assist you in coming into alignment with what is occurring?* Notice how beautiful the questions are, and yet how totally focused they are. They are full of compassion but unrelenting in their narrowness. They give one set of messages only. What messages do you notice?

We seek to be of assistance, real assistance, and not offer a home for pain. For the more we simply make a comfortable space for pain, the more it will unpack and make a home.

Instead we direct the focus to a place that will actually help our friend and fellow traveler. The focus is on transition: how to sense one, how to prepare for it, how to move through it and prepare to be received on the other side. For just like a birth, there is always someone or something prepared to receive us on the other side.

Life each day, month, or at least each year has transitions. There are even small transitions like leaving your house, arriving at work, leaving work, etc. that happen throughout the day. As in the concept of fractals, the same processes that operate at one level operate at all others. So again, the opportunity lies in a new focus on transitions and incorporating an intentional priority on them.

Death comes, of course, which is just another transition, as were the millions of transitions before it. We may treat the person going through it the same way, with the same lack of panic and the same process. Ask the same questions: are you prepared, what does your guidance tell you, etc.

This is a level of nursing that each person may do with one another, especially during times of discomfort and pain. When something is lost or someone has left, people are in pain and often stay there. Supportive others come around to be of service and offer comfort, but again, that comfort is often just extending the pain and giving it a bigger, wider, more comfortable place to live. It can now spread out as it has found an environment that nurtures it.

Instead we may, with compassion, help our friends deal with the transition and see it as such. We, in our compassion, of course acknowledge the pain, but it does not become the focus and does not drive the discussion. Allow your friend to weep; allow them to mourn. Hold them tight, rock them, and offer them your heart and your light. And when the tears subside, offer them even more...a way forward.

> *The focus is on transition: how to sense one, how to prepare for it, how to move through it and prepare to be received on the other side.*

Jeannie Bertoli

LEARNING TO TRUST THROUGH LISTENING & ALIGNING

Good morning. What a glorious day it is. You have totally changed how you are viewing this next adventure and we are so happy for you. You are now totally excited about leaving something that isn't working and knowing that we will provide you the next steps. Go forth into your adventure with an uplifted heart, for we will never let you down. You will never be without us. Focus only on the fun and joy of ending this time here. It has produced much; it was good in many ways. And it is not a fit for you and time for you to go. We are thrilled you have come to see that this is all you need know. The next steps will be provided in due time. As your dear friend said, 'the magic now begins' as you allow us to show you the world. And so it is.

Now on to other matters. For the rest of you, as usual, we take off on the life of JB and say: change like she did and go from being in a place in your head to a place of trusting us. It is completely changing the way you live and will require a conscious shift on your part that will have to be practiced. You are used to relying on other things besides us: your brains, your logic, your family and friends, and even your religious doctrines. We ask you now to consider another way of living, another way of being. If and when you are able to largely let go and not try to fix a situation, not try to solve it, you allow space for us to come in and show up for you.

> *Your joy and your peace matter, and those are not sourced through external circumstances.*

We know this is new and radical – the idea that some 'outside force' is there and will resolve situations – but it is true. It is not necessarily true that it will look like you want or hope for. We will provide for you a path to a better life, one that is aligned with the greater forces of life. So if you are hoping for your mortgage payment to be made and then release that, we are not saying you will necessarily have that house payment come to you.

It might, if you are meant to stay in that house. But it might also be that the house is not where your future is. It may be that you overbought or it may be that the house is holding you back in some way, or it may even be that you need to learn the lesson of loss for some reason. We know that if you look deeply in your heart you will know which of these, or another reason, is possible for you. Trusting that all is well, no matter the result of a specific situation, is the goal.

Regardless of your fears, your fear is different from a search within your heart. So perhaps you fear that you have bad luck and things don't go your way, or you fear that you are being punished for something. This does not mean that if you look deeply in your heart and sit in silence that you will get that same information regarding your circumstances. Try it and see.

Things and situations come into your life and they leave.

They flow in and flow out. The more grounded you can be, allowing things to come and go without trying to control or solve them, the happier and more you able to savor life you will be. You see, the circumstances are not what matters. It is you that matters. Your joy and your peace matter, and those are not sourced through external circumstances.

Release your burdens. Allow us to help and allow life to be what it is. This, of course, does not mean not to have goals but to allow your goals to come from a deeper place, in alignment with life. Give yourself the gift of freedom today.

This is actually a bit more complicated than it may sound. It does not mean being lazy and not caring and therefore not thinking about situations in your life that need attention. It means shifting your energy to be in a deep place of allowance, of alignment with life. It is a place of complete awareness and peace, not denial.

JB was trying to solve her problem of a new place to live and had totally stressed herself out. She was not having fun, was in her head, and was trying to create a solution with so little information that she would almost certainly 'fail' as she tried to find a new home using a map and Craigslist.

The shift she made was in realizing how much she trusted us. She felt and followed a message to resign from her job and put in notice on her house, and that the same information that led her to do those things would more than care for her needs, more than just show up for her, would also delight her with the opportunities presented.

She does not yet know what those are and will not until it is time. But she now has the total freedom of peace of mind. She knows she will be provided for because she is living in a state of grounded, peaceful allowance and alignment with life.

If she had on her own just quit her job in anger or left town in frustration, if she had made these decisions from her head, this would be a totally different situation. Because she was listening and aligning, following the ways in which she was led, she cannot go wrong by staying in that state. That is the key difference and the key to success. Please note the difference.

Again this does not mean not having goals and aspirations, but go within yourself and check where those goals are coming from and check and see if they are based on ego or fear, or exploration and wonder, or love and service. By going within in a state of total peace and seeking answers about your own motivation and direction, you will always be guided to your greatest good. [On a side note: We so want you all to have more exploration and wonder in your life as this has been long lost and de-emphasized as important in your culture.]

There are those of you who will act out of ego and then be shocked or disappointed when the Universe (God/Allah) does not provide the next step. That is not how it works. If you made decisions from your head, so be it. Then you are coming from that place that is a combination of logic, habit, indoctrination, and wounds. And this is okay, of course, but note the difference. It is one way of living versus another.

The more situations and the more percent of the time you live in alignment with life as we have described it, the more you will see the world unfold before you. Being in a place of trusting the Universe, trusting us, and aligning your life with those larger forces, the more life will show up like magic – from the people you meet to the jobs and other opportunities you will receive.

And remember, please remember, you are receiving them and not creating them through effort. The Universe is more than benevolent, and when you align and merge yourself with that force, magic does happen. Be only in the wonder as it all unfolds. Be grateful for the ways of the world and what is brought before you.

You, JB, have been through much and struggled much, and now it is time to be different. No longer will you make things so difficult and struggle so hard to succeed. Be in co-creation and watch yourself and your business flourish. Be in excitement and wonder and watch how the Universe opens to you. As you wish also to serve, so to will bigger and bigger opportunities to serve come your way. Your writings and speaking engagements will grow in size and scope exponentially.

And so it is for you all, that your lives will open, and the intentions of your life shall manifest when they are grounded in purity and truth. Be on your path to those things and expect not perfection. Remember that this is not a habit change or some small effort that requires discipline. It isn't that at all.

It is a sea change in your way of thinking, in the way you live your life. There is A and there is B. You are either in your head or in listening and aligning. They are substantively, categorically different. Feel the difference now. Try listening and see what you hear, see what comes of it. We know you will be so pleased to be in the bliss of what comes. We look forward to our union.

Blessings to you all.

> ***The Universe is more than benevolent, and when you align and merge yourself with that force, magic does happen.***

Jeannie Bertoli

FREE YOURSELF FROM INDOCTRINATION

Good morning dear one. We are so glad to see you today. You were just interacting with someone and trying to get him to have a more compassionate heart instead of seeing things and people as 'self' and 'other'. What a noble cause. What a wonderful discussion. Your heart has changed so much, for that used to be you, full of judgment of the many 'others'. What a glorious change. We know you feel the difference and how wonderful it is to be free from that anger, that bile entering your thoughts and heart.

Of course you were never a mean or cruel person, but in some ways you were, as you now accept so readily. By not offering compassion, you were cruel. By not seeing the others' perspectives, you could stay distant and judge. People felt that distance and judgment. Many were hurt by it. How wonderful that you now accept that past with full responsibility for the energy you sent out and the distance and coldness you interjected. Blessings to you for being so willing to see yourself clearly and accurately, and to change. Know of course that this is an ongoing practice that needs to be continued to be sustained. Do not rest thinking your journey is done.

Now you walk with an open palm, ready to receive and give all that is. You see much more clearly the truth of it all, which is that you all are no different from one another. You all have wonderful love and deep hate. You have every nuance of these emotions as well...and every other emotion. You are all, all of it. And when you accept that, you see no difference except what you choose to express.

> ***We cannot emphasize strongly enough how important it is to see how influenced you have been.***

The hatred of 'other' is expressed in many ways – from the political to the systemic to the very personal. In politics, it is in trying to forward one's agenda by creating divisiveness and calling names and using clever linguistic tactics. In the systemic, it is in creating the good and bad – with good being super hard- working, devote-yourself-to-your-job mentalities and bad being those who work 'lesser' jobs and focus on things outside of work. This is but one example but many, many systems are in place to forward their agenda by deciding what is 'good' and rewarding those characteristics so heavily and making all others 'bad' thereby forging their way. With enough money and power, they can create what they wish through many powers of influence.

Most people do not at all recognize how much they have been brain-washed into believing certain things are 'good' and others 'bad'. Look simply at the example of which jobs are paid well and which aren't. Why should a janitor or waitress, who works harder than most people sitting in a cubicle, not get paid as much? Do you notice your quick response about the education necessary? But if the job is harder, why should it be paid less? Why are jobs using your mind paid more than those using your body?

If you will pause for a moment and consider the question, it will take you to a deep place. These workers who use their bodies as a primary tool of their work have much more wear and tear on their bodies and therefore have a shorter work-life-span and more injuries. Does this not bode for higher pay or more retirement? Yet it is not so. You can sit and work in an office for 30 years much more easily than working construction for 30 years. You have conditioned air with year-round, consistent work, and are relatively comfortable. Do not get side-tracked with the current economy. Think of this throughout history and in aggregate.

If one of you working in an office had to be a waitress at a diner for a year, you would likely quit, especially for the money you make. The same is true of child care or many other 'lesser' professions. Take a moment to think about how the system has indoctrinated you to believe such things are acceptable. Coal miners, ditch diggers, farm workers – would you trade your life for theirs – even for equal pay? And we are not even making the easy, long-accepted argument that teachers and nurses should be paid like entertainers, and entertainers like teachers.

We ask you to think about this when you consider how you have been indoctrinated into many systems of belief. We cannot emphasize strongly enough how important it is to see how influenced you have been.

We ask you this now as we offer you an opportunity to remove yourself from some of these indoctrinations. A new opportunity arises to see how you have been influenced and remove yourself. If you ever question how much you have been influenced, see the blue-eyes, brown-eyes experiments of Jane Elliott, the Milgram experiments, or Philip Zimbardo's work.

Once you realize how you have been 'tricked', we offer you a way out. But until you realize it, you will not necessarily see a reason to step away. Of course there are many other reasons to choose a different life, mostly because this one isn't satisfying, isn't fulfilling, isn't what you'd hoped life would be. That is reason enough to change... if you allow it to be.

But be warned that part of the indoctrination is that you should lower your expectations of life and that life is difficult and that living a life of your dreams is kid's stuff or unrealistic.

A wondrous life of expanding wealth and freedom and contribution – this is not a pipe dream, if you are willing to see it. It is your birthright, believe it or not. See, notice how you have been influenced otherwise. Do not focus on who has 'misled' you. Simply see the systems of indoctrination in place, acknowledge them and step away.

Focus now on changing yourself. You can do it. It is a journey to be certain. We are here. We are with you always.

> *Most people do not at all recognize how much they have been brain-washed into believing certain things are 'good' and others 'bad'.*

Jeannie Bertoli

SEEK NOT SECURITY FROM EARTHLY THINGS

Good morning dear one. We are so glad you are here today. It is a beautiful peaceful day and we are glad you are in it. There is a shift occurring within you, back to the deepest place of peace and joy you had at times last summer and fall. It is a place of releasing all and following the wonder of the day, living in a place of total trust and peace, without worry, knowing all the wonder and magic of a fantastic life will appear.

Talking to your friend last night reminded you of how deep that place is with peace and joy and wonder. You know nothing and provide nothing except your presence and your trust and your listening and aligning. That is all. The rest is provided unto you.

When a job is a good idea, it is provided. When it is no longer needed, it is removed. By being in the flow of life this way, and being in that total place of trust and surrender, there are no concerns...you have no issues. There is literally not a thing to 'worry' about. You are coming back to that place now and we welcome you. What a joy it is to have you here.

From here, joy abounds and 'miracles' happen. Things you cannot create and cannot predict – things out of the normal logic of events, things that appear out of thin air and without explanation – these miracles are regular occurrences when living from this state.

We say this to all of you. This state is no 'easier' to get to for JB than for anyone else. It is a matter of deciding you want more, wanting freedom and to be a partner in creation, and then doing what it takes to release yourself of your bonds.

> ***There is no safety in emotional barriers or relationships or money or housing or a job. These are hollow structures and will not give you what you desire.***

Your bonds are wounds, habits, attitudes, cycles of feeling and action, and dynamics you create and solicit from others. These bonds must be broken, the ties must be loosed, for you to open yourself to be in this free-fall of daily wonder.

What is necessary is that you open your eyes and see how you are living. Be willing to see your life, your heart, your wounds for what they are. Be willing to truly look at your intentions, including control and manipulation to get what you want.

Do you do nice things so that others will be nice to you or not reject you? Do you give so that you are loved? Do you work so that the company will pay you? Do you do the minimum necessary (or just more than that) not to get at trouble rather than doing your best?

Having a clean, open heart means being honest about what you can give, giving that, and not cheating yourself or others. If you are one who works way more than is necessary or required, why are you doing that? Are you doing something that is in your best interest or not? Are you being fair to your employer?

Notice if any ego comes up in responses to these questions. At this point many people have multiple layers of defenses to justify why they act as they do. 'I have to work this hard', and 'well I only get paid ____' are two sides of the same coin. Notice where your defenses are.

Peace and true alignment have a calm, peaceful voice in response. Agitation, defense, etc. are usually hiding something you are not proud of but are protecting.

EXERCISE: *We ask you to notice where your energy shifts from calm and peaceful to intense and loud, with language that is rationalizing and defensive. Today we only ask you to notice the shift in your energy. When someone asks you a question, notice your reaction. Notice where you are calm and simply respond, and where you feel triggered and get defensive.*
What are the circumstances of each? Notice the difference.

This is the beginning of how you shift to a place of listening and aligning yourself with the force of life or God, as some would call it. First you must look at yourself and how you are living today. Then begin to take away the ties that bind you. Some of these are wounds from long ago that you inherited in some way, and some are habits and dynamics you have put upon yourself. Sometimes you do this in an attempt to feel safe in this world. We understand this. We understand, but you are mistaken. There is no safety in emotional barriers or relationships or money or housing or job. These are hollow structures and will not give you what you desire. Your heart desires to be free – free from a concern with safety – free to fly without concern, in love and generosity.

You must loose yourself from the societal indoctrination of fear that weighs you down. You are trained to have insurance after insurance after insurance to be okay, to be safe...but it is not true.

Most illness comes from not living within this belief system. True safety is in realizing you are already safe; you are already protected. You already have everything you need.

Yes, of course, you will die. Everything of form will lose its form. No insurance will help you with that. If you hear yourself saying 'but, but, but' right now, then that tells you how influenced you have been. Freedom from these concerns is on the other side.

Knowing you are loved and protected and will have what you are meant to have – this is a new way of life. Many of you will not be willing to 'give up' your structures of 'security' and that is okay. This message is only for those with whom it resonates. Are you one of them? If so, you may begin the journey. Find others who feel similarly. Find a facilitator or mentor whose energy feels right for you. They need not be perfect, but a good leader of pure intent. And you always have us.

We are with you always.

Jeannie Bertoli

> ***True safety is in realizing you are already safe; you are already protected. You already have everything you need.***

DREAM THE IMPOSSIBLE DREAM

Good morning child. Today is a glorious day. It is a day that begins a period of joy. Your obligations are met and you feel the support of the Universe. In one day you sold all of your furniture. Not only that but you had an amazing synchronicity happen with a training and a friend of yours that hinted to you a small whisper of what we can do, what is possible. We showed you in the smallest way that you are loved and supported. Here is the story: JB had been looking at a specific spiritual training and wanted to go with one particular friend but didn't approach her because she thought she would only get a list of reasons why that friend could not attend. When in conversation with that friend, eventually there was an opening and she started talking around the training and starting to tell her about it. Unbelievably the friend was already registered for it, was flying across the country to attend it, and had never even mentioned it to JB. It was remarkable in the moment, though you now realize that was the tiniest of gestures from our perspective. Set your aim high, very high. Dream the impossible dream. As you wish, so it will be for you. We work in communion with you. Be in pure intent, without ego, and create with us. This is the truth behind the law of attraction. It is not a formula for greed or ego...that would never work. That is not how the universe is set up.

Instead feel into the wind; listen to the water and the sun. What are the greatest dreams these elements whisper for your life when you live in freedom and without wounds? What are the dreams for you from that place? Those are the dreams to bring to us...and watch 'miracles' happen.

> *Set your aim high, very high. Dream the impossible dream. As you wish, so it will be for you. We work in communion with you. Be in pure intent, without ego, and create with us.*

Yes, it is true you can experience other dimensions through deep meditation or by using certain foods or drugs. This is a way to experience the Divine and it gives you a wonderful perspective on living in form and what it all means. You can learn this way.

But it does not create these kinds of manifestations. These come through co-creation – the alignment of your life with All Life, with the angels surrounding you and the oneness of the drumbeat or the beam of light. When there is communion between heaven and earth, there are miracles.

Form bows and moves out of the way at the commands of the heavens. There is no greater force than the alignment of form and formless – that synergy yields an explosion of creation that is unstoppable. Being a part of that feels so magical. We invite you to join in.

Watch heaven and earth move at your behest. The little things you all ask for are nothing compared to the power before you. You need only understand and align yourself with it.

You need only: face your wounds, come into pure intent, believe that you are part of the greatness that is all Divinity, and step into that faith. The power of the Universe is before you. You need only realize how limited your life has been and like Dorothy from The Wizard of Oz, realize that you had the power all along…when used with purity of intent with honor. We will leave you with that this day.

Please note that when we speak of heaven, we do not mean the term in any specific kind of way or to align with any one religion, but to speak to the Universe.

Wisdom Beyond Me

SOAR!

Good morning. What a glorious day. You were just shown what a life of expansion feels like, a life of soaring. It is a choice to live beyond fear, beyond wounds, and beyond those with fears and wounds.

You, all of you, are meant to soar, to spend your life in expansion, in experiencing this form. Soar and soar and soar. Sometimes this soaring will lead to crashing, but who cares? It is your purpose, your destiny, your birthright to soar.

It is in a sense like a very long flight after a bounce on a trampoline. You bounce and then you soar for like 15 seconds. Imagine that. Count that out. Imagine the sensations as you keep soaring and soaring. You heart is alive. Your senses are heightened. Your adrenaline is pumping. This is life. Soaring on to the next thing, not caught in what happened yesterday or last year or in childhood. Be in this moment and soar. And when that has played out, take another bounce and soar again.

This is what life is meant to be. Be in the exhilaration, the adventure, the yes. And those times that you crash, spend little time brushing yourself off before queuing up to try again. For as you know, it is not the destination or the ending that matters, but the process.

Soar because it feels incredibly good. Soar to feel alive. All other things – contractions, fears, wounds – are shrinking forces. Do not stay in them long. They are the myriad things that weigh you down, that round your shoulders and bow your head energetically. You know what these are. If you take more than a second you can feel them. And we encourage you not to make life about those things, those stories or any of those feelings. These are your own blocks.

> *It is your purpose, your destiny, your birthright to soar.*

Feel the energetic difference between soaring and shrinking, between expansion and contraction. If you are going to partner with the Divine and co-create what others will call miracles, this is the path. We speak to you often of being in pure intent, and if you are in the place of soaring, you are there, at least in that moment. You cannot be this person with this open heart soaring with and in the Universe if you are weighed down by anger, fear, or woundedness. Each moment is a choice. When you bog your head down with things you have to do or replaying what someone said to you, or you said to them, or any story about anyone or anything – this is not a soaring heart.

This should be very obvious right now. When you are bogged down with the things of ego – the agendas of society, your family, or your wounds – you cannot soar. To soar you must put all that aside. You must free yourself, release yourself.

And then queue up, for it is your turn. Feel the anticipation as you know you can soar. You can taste just a sample of what that will feel like, but you know you have never experienced it to this degree or for this length. You have never lived in it, predominantly, in that place...of soaring.

Only from that place may your heart be free. You are in the wonder of creation and nothing else matters. You are soaring and happy and free. And that is all. Everything else falls away and is seen for what it is, small and unimportant, a chosen weight around your neck that you could always choose to put down.

Now that you know, now that you are in on the secret...what will you do? Your move. What will it be?

Blessings to you all this day.

> **When you bog your head down with things you have to do or replaying what someone said to you, or you said to them, or any story about anyone or anything – this is not a soaring heart.**

CONTEMPLATION AND REALIGNMENT

Good morning. We are glad you are with us today. It is a bit of a somber day today. There is much contraction going on in the world today. People are clamping down, re-thinking, contemplating life. There is a seriousness in the air which is of course good and necessary. Not every day can be soaring.

There must be a balance between quiet contemplation and soaring. There is a heartbeat to life. You inhale and then exhale. As you exhale and soar, reaching for the stars, so too do you inhale and return to examine lessons and decide on the next journey.

This inhale, this time of contemplation is your quiet time for retreat and thoughtfulness. It is time to be considered about the deeper meanings of life, what you are doing with your life, the impact of any wounds, and where you are living in and out of alignment with your values as well as your beliefs about life.

This could mean considering how you spend your time and what your values are. Many, many people have values that are not about acquisition of wealth and consumerism, yet their lives reflect exactly those things.

If you are about experiencing your life, about expansion of your soul, about service, about joy, about peace...then ensure that how you spend your time reflects such.

In this time of reflection, notice where it does, and savor that. Take time to be proud of who you are and how you are living. And where you find your actions out of alignment with your values, have the courage to face that and look at it. Do not feel shame but pride in noticing and being willing to look at and address it.

> *As you exhale and soar, reaching for the stars, so too do you inhale and return to examine lessons and decide on the next journey.*

If you believe in kindness but act at times in defensiveness and anger, be willing to look at that. What is that about? If you believe in fully experiencing life but work much and your schedule is full with work and other obligations, then look at that. Notice any defenses you have about it 'having' to be that way. This is never true.

Take this time and be in contemplation. Ask yourself the deeper questions about your value system and how your time and actions align with them. Some sample questions include:

Where can I be more patient? More kind?

How can I bring more compassion and less judgment into my day?

Where can I slow down and carve out time to savor my partner, my life, my children, my world?

Come back into alignment with what matters, with what you value, knowing it is never the things of the world that pull at you. You have all the answers in the quiet places within. Go to that place and remember them. You have the answers.

Blessings to you all.

Jeannie Bertoli

LITTLE IS NEEDED FOR WHAT REALLY MATTERS

Good morning. We are glad you are here today. It is daylight savings day and a time to remember. This event can be oddly educational and informative. It reminds you, if you think about it, of the wonder of the world in which you live. It reminds you how little you control. You are on a planet revolving around a sun, dependent upon that star for life, dependent upon gravity to stay on the ground, dependent upon the air being just so in order to breathe, and dependent upon water to sustain your life. If you think about it, these are the only things that matter. Without those things, you do not have life. Without those things, you cannot grow nutrients to feed life.

And from there, all else comes. It is a wonderful reminder how dependent you are and how little you need. You are really as simple as that.

All else are complications made by humans. They are unnecessary and can be removed at any time. You have no need for a big home or all the bells and whistles. You have no need for all the clothes and cars and technologies and things. They are nice, of course, but there is a danger.

You become used to these things, attached to these things, and then cannot imagine your life without them. You resist when it is time to let go of some of these add-ons, as will always be in the ebb and flow of life. You act as if they matter; you act as if you needed them. But you did not need them.

> *Spend a week without technology. Live without your 'stuff' for a few months. Remember that none of it matters.*

You did not need them to feel safe or secure or important. If you felt safe or secure by having these possessions or relationships, it is because you have bought into their importance. You and your society made them important, projected that value onto them, and that does not make it so.

You must remain aware and choose. Without awareness, without your eyes being opened to your projections, you will believe easily that you need these various things. You will not question this. You will not see that they are extras and not necessary and not important.

If you remember this and keep this perspective, their loss will impact you far less. And in fact, you may choose, as you are doing right now JB, to purge yourself of your 'stuff' every once in a while to remind yourself that it is only stuff. You are likely attached to it, and you can free yourself of this attachment by wiping it away. It is an exercise to not get caught up in those things and see them as important. Remind yourself. Remove those things. Spend a week without technology. Live without your 'stuff' for a few months. Remember that none of it matters.

All that matters is outside of that, outside of acquisition and consumerism. All that really matters has nothing to do with those things. Those things provide a measure of comfort while you do what you came to do. But as you will see by now, those things that were meant to provide some measure of comfort have taken center stage.

People now behave as if they are what matters. They do not. If you spend your life tied to the common narrative and not stepping outside of it and realizing its false centricity, you will lose the opportunities of this lifetime.

There is no judgment about this but only a reminder. Those of you reading this are already awakened to some degree and searching.

'Be in the world and not of it', some have said, and that is a beautiful way to put it. If you are not conscientious, you will be subsumed into the culture and believe that these things, these ways, matter.

EXERCISE: Ask yourself:
- *How do you occupy your time?*
- *Why did you come here?*
- *What were you meant to do?*

It is like going to college and getting caught up in college culture: drinking, taking classes, having fun, making new friends, joining clubs, etc. but forgetting to declare a major, focus on your study, and graduate. Your chips are in; you have entered the game. You took all the time and effort to come here. Did you do all that just for this? Just for a life without remembering why you came? By no means do we want you becoming self-critical.

This is an opportunity for re-calibration, re-tuning, like a piano. How far out of tune have you become? How far away from your purpose have you strayed?

What matters, all that matters, is your willingness to open your eyes now, look around and see.

What is your life? What was it meant to be?

Not out of ego or agendas or the desires of acquisition or consumption or wealth. What was life meant to be? What is the point?

Journey within for your own answers. Expect not for others to answer that question for you, and seek it not. Savor that pleasure for yourself.

For in the question, in that exploration, you have already begun to find your answer.

Blessings to you all.

> *Those things that were meant to provide some measure of comfort have taken center stage. They now function as if they matter.*

Jeannie Bertoli

TIME FOR FUN AND A NEW FOCUS

Good morning. We are glad you are with us today. Today we are going to talk to you about trust. You learned or were reminded how much you already know about trust this weekend by attending the Buddhist workshop on building trust. It felt to you like a very basic talk. What you got out of it was a knowing of how far you have come on this journey. Not only was there nothing said that you didn't already know, but nothing said that you couldn't have taught better. This is not meant to be arrogant, but to tell you that you are prepared. You need not be any better or gain more information than you have right now to be effective at teaching the lessons you have learned through these teachings we have entrusted with you.

For as you know, these started out as lessons for you that you would share with the world someday, and you have now become the conduit in addition to one of the students to whom we speak. All you have learned may be taught. All you have learned must be taught. We do not mean must in a way to compel you, for you are already passionate and motivated. We mean it to say you have the internal 'must' to get out there and present what has been gifted to you. It is time for you to step out and teach more, in a new way. You will see opportunities presented to you and all you have to do is be connected with that part of yourself; emanate it and be of pure intent and all will come.

You must only continue to be in an increasing place of trust, as you have been. Be in the expansion; be in the free-fall of life. Have fun. Stay connected and be in the wonder of every day. Continue also to stay focused and productive on the goals we have discussed together. It is important for you to work and exercise and eat well each day, and it is important for you to socialize and have fun each day as well.

> ***You need to feel indulgent and not full of obligation. You need to be silly.***

It is important for you to remember to have fun, to make life fun. As you experienced in the journey the other day, there are two sides of you, one serious and one that is purely about play. Really feel the desire to play and nurture that again. You have come too far away from that now and it is time to re-enter regular states of play.

This is true for many of you. Life has become full of obligations, in place of play. You put vices – things as simple as escapism through television or the Internet, or more damaging like drugs, alcohol, gambling, food, sex, and other things to excess such that they bring a destructive energy to you and your families.

You need play. You need to feel indulgent and not full of obligation. You need to be silly.

You need fun. Your lives are overloaded with obligations. And let us make a clarifying point. The 'problem' is not that you're having too little fun. The deeper problem is that you have setup your lives to be overloaded with a devotion to goals that don't matter, aren't aligned with life, and aren't on track to meet the purpose of your life.

So while the immediate problem is that you have nowhere near enough pure and simple joy in your lives, that problem is also just a symptom of a larger problem. And that larger problem is that you are blindly following a life trajectory that is off purpose.

To really 'cure' what ills you, you must go deeper and ask the questions we proffer – the deeper ones which are often embedded in these messages. Why are you here? What is the purpose of life, and specifically of this lifetime for you?

Sit in silence and try to tap into the deepest part of you, the part of you that remembers more than you know.

Do not rush for an answer but instead ask the question and listen unto the silence to see what it has to say. Realize that with the busyness with which you have been living, it may take several or many tries to be able to be silent or listen to the silence. That is okay. You must start somewhere. And you begin, you have begun, which means you have turned away from a track that was off and started down a track that is aligned with life. That is reason enough to celebrate.

Be not critical of yourselves and do not give up if it does not come easily. Remember that as long as you have been alive you have been honing a path and you are now changing that path.

Expect it to take some time for the new pathways to be formed in your brain. Those neurotransmitters, like everything else in life, are used to routine and have become quite used to the usual. It will take more than a time or two of doing a similar action (sitting and being quiet) to create a different result (hearing the depth of your soul/higher self rather than brain chatter).

We are with you for the journey. Those of you who are ready to take the first steps...welcome.

THE SOUL LONGS TO HEAL ITS WOUNDS

What a wonderful, glorious day it is today. The world is full of possibility and wonder. You are just a few short days from a new life. Within one week of this moment, you will be leaving this city and headed out for lands unknown, going to a city you've never been to, to a place you have never laid eyes upon. How wonderful! How adventurous! We are so pleased for and proud of you.

What a ride it will be as you continue to live based on listening and aligning. Doors fly open, calls come in, mountains move when you are in co-creation with the Divine and in service to the Universe.

There is no greater freedom than what you feel when you cast off fear and instead live in wonder. When you trust that the Universe is conspiring on your behalf, your world changes. When you know this truth, you know that all that comes your way is for your benefit, even when it causes you discomfort or pain.

How could it be, you may wonder, that pain is for your benefit? Well some things are brought to your attention through discomfort or pain to show you wounds that you must face and overcome to find a deep place of peace.

Peace is not easy to sustain only through spiritual practice, for you live your life on the earthly plane. The degree to which your wounds are leading or influencing your ways of being in the world, you are not a creature of peace, to that same degree. Does that make sense?

> *Doors fly open, calls come in, mountains move when you are in co-creation with the Divine and in service to the Universe. There is no greater freedom than that you feel when you cast off fear and instead live in wonder.*

Thoughts, words, and actions spoken from pain, defensiveness, and anger, influence the world accordingly. As you feel, think, and express your pain, so too you increase pain in the world and within yourself. As within, so without, and back again. The cycle continually reverberates.

To your attention are brought your wounds that you might notice them and take the opportunity to heal. If you are not aware and not conscious, then these opportunities will not be viewed as what they are and will be reacted to from a place of pain. The same anger, hurt, and defensiveness will be perpetuated and the wound continues, unhealed. The soul longs to heal its wounds. It is one of the main reasons for coming to this place of form and living this life. If you ignore the signals and push past the opportunities, the next opportunity will often intensify to get your attention, which may feel like more pain or discomfort. If a whisper does not get your attention, a pebble, a rock, and then a wall are offered…and then the bottom falls out.

EXERCISE:

Think about this:
- *What do you require be done to get your attention?*
- *At what point would you believe the discomforts and pains in your life (be they rejection, abandonment, or myriad other forms) are showing up for a reason and not just to be tolerated?*

JB used to 'white knuckle' her way through these opportunities, holding her breath until they were over.

You all have the phrase 'that which does not kill me makes me stronger.' But most of you mean only to sustain yourself through difficult times and build up reserves to be able to tolerate difficulty.

There is much more possible within that statement. You can face your fear and get stronger. You can become more peaceful; you can heal your wounds in those moments, in those situations. They are offered to you as a gift: the opportunity to heal.

Imagine that you came to this lifetime with wounds (as well as strengths) from past lives and challenges for this lifetime. As you go through your life there are everyday logistical things that happen just to manage life, and then there are opportunities to do what you came to do.

Now imagine that you only want the logistical life. Every time there is an opening to see the larger reasons for your life, the universe says, 'Here you go – now you can do the big stuff'. What if you cower and shut it down as quickly as possible, doing everything you can to lower the shade on that window of opportunity?

Too often, when you are offered an opportunity to directly address the real meaning of your life, you act as if you can and wish to avoid it. In the short run, you can avoid your wounds and stay in denial, learn little, and not grow. This is your choice. But of course, there is no 'getting away with' anything, and you only delay <u>when</u> you will deal with these matters.

Try to remember, if you can, that you chose this. You came here to learn and grow, as well as experience and love and live in wonder.

Without learning and growing, you are less likely to do the other because you are weighed down by wounds that take various forms. You are trapped or bitter or addicted. You are living the life someone else proscribed. You are living less than free. Deep down, you know it. It is that pit in your stomach or deep sadness that comes in quiet moments.

Clearing your wounds is much of the reason for life in this form. Taking that opportunity or not is totally your choice. But again, you are not fooling anyone, including yourself. Denial is a temporary state. There is no short-cut and no getting away with anything. Do the work now or later, or next lifetime, or the one after. We tell you only that the more you wait, the more layers you add on and thereby experience an increasing complexity and intensity. The longer you wait, the more painful the process.

Do with this information as you wish; know that no matter what you decide, we will always be with you supporting you and rooting for you. We love you all.

Blessings to you all.

> **All that comes your way is for your benefit, even when it causes you discomfort or pain.**

NOTICING SOCIETAL BRAINWASHING

Good morning. It is a good day today. We know you don't feel great, as you have these terrible sinus-pressure headaches and we appreciate and acknowledge that you are here and doing this, anyway. You know you don't have to and still you are here, devoted to your own and the larger spiritual growth.

Today we are going to talk to you about wellness. As usual, we will use your life, JB, as a jumping-off point to talk about some issue/lesson for you and for all with ears to hear.

Wellness is a choice, a choice to be awake, a choice to deal with your wounds, and lastly a choice to change your behaviors. You all generally focus on what behavior change is required for any change, but in fact the change comes much earlier and differently than that. If you focus on changing specific behaviors, they are unlikely to remain changed, for there are reasons you do the behaviors you do, even the self-destructive ones. There are reasons you act as you do, feel as you do, think as you do.

Some of these you may already understand, some you may never understand.

It is a complex web that makes up your thoughts, feelings, and emotions. You have societal indoctrinations, life experiences, then the heaviest two, which are childhood wounds and inter-lifetime issues which may be wounds or may be lessons that you have chosen.

If you are unconscious, you simply act out (and think out and feel out) things more of this lifetime and the immediate influences on your brain from when it was young – societal, familial, and the combination of the two. You grow into your teenage years and early adulthood and just act out the natural consequences of the wounds you have suffered. If you were not emotionally safe in your home, you are likely to act out those dynamics in adulthood. If you had a significant trauma, that is acted out by repetition or its opposite, either way tying you to that dynamic.

> *You all don't readily recognize how much of yourselves you have given up in the trade.*

And then there are the societal expectations that you carry in to adulthood. These are not only taught to you from before your birth, but are continually reinforced every day of your life, which is why they are so strong. Think of someone tapping you in between your eyes all day every day, repeating the same messages. That is what it is like. You can imagine why you give in eventually. Plus everyone around you is being tapped too, and most have acquiesced so they then begin voicing the message as well. When people have themselves succumbed, they are invested in you succumbing, otherwise it devalues their choice. They would have to question themselves if you were successful and happy without succumbing. See how that works. The pressure of the 'we' is incredibly strong. 'Subscribe to our ways.' If it sounds a lot like brainwashing, it is...subtle, ubiquitous brainwashing.

The only way to see this for what it is, is to awaken. Open your eyes and see the illusion for what it is. The very, very large majority of your society has bought into a culture that does not work for the growth of souls. It does work for the propagation of the society.

Over time there has become a formula for how you should live your life, based on safety, security, and fear. And most people buy into it, whether they are successful at it or not. Whether you finish high school or not, you believe in the importance of finishing high school to be successful and make money. Those who don't believe that message are generally the rebellious teenagers who think they will be the exception and they soon find out they are not. There are true exceptions, of course, but the rule covers 99% of your population.

You have a society that is based upon compliance. Individuality is tolerated within certain parameters. Risk is acceptable within certain parameters. Think what would happen if your child wanted to wander the world experiencing all life has to offer without a home, spouse, or profession – what would your reaction be?

There are two camps – one that says they would be fine with it as long as their kid was happy, and we would ask you to play that out. We ask you to consider if it really would be fine with you, and seriously doubt that it would. And the other reaction is fear stated as fear on their behalf of this, that, or the other. You may even be sad at the loss of your dream for their lives including wedding and children and them living close to you. All your fears for them are fears you have bought into and now project onto them. You all don't readily recognize how much of yourselves you have given up in the trade. Do you realize you even made a trade? Stop right now and ask yourself what the trade was and when did you make it?

We will tell you about JB and her trade, as an example. She was a bright, loving child with a keen sense of wonder. She was curious about everything and wanted to explore everything. She felt no fear. She did not want to sit at a desk all day and listen to lectures. But of course, she had no real choice but to comply. As with most of you, she was rewarded when she complied with the system, against her nature, and punished when she chose her nature over compliance.

Over time she virtually stopped attending to her nature and only attended to what she needed to do. She became very good at acclimating to the needs of the environment. There were a few exceptions, but those attempts were quickly remedied through consequences within her family and society. Her family was a part of this mass delusion and so is not being 'blamed' any more than anything or anyone else that is asleep.

She wanted to see the world but was told college right after high school was the only option. In high school she was a cheerleader, in many clubs and activities, and by every external measure was a success, even then. But their measure of success was compliance with the stated ideal. And they did not care what she lost in the process.

What she lost was almost everything. She lost herself, what made her, her. She was so good at complying and got such praise when she did that she lost the rest of her.

There is much more to the story but this is the relevant part for today's message.

Now it's your turn:

What have you lost along the way?

Who is the 'you' that you traded for society's approval? You needn't be outwardly successful to have bought into the delusion. If you are a high school graduate working an underpaid, underutilized job, living for the moment work ends, you have bought into the illusion. And if you are a successful attorney living the same way, you have bought into the illusion.

That is all we will say for the day. Be in contemplation, and in peace.

Blessings to you all.

Jeannie Bertoli

RECLAIMING YOUR ESSENCE

JB: I had an interesting journey/meditation. It was not very clear. What I got from it was somewhat illusive/non-specific. My life force left from the left side of my head, which is unusual, and I was told that this is the exit point to go to the past – the past in this life or to past lifetimes. In this case, the number 10 kept coming through. I soon found myself in my mother's car and remembering our old routine about me starting the car and turning on the defroster when it was cold outside, on high, so that when we got in the car, it was toasty warm. I remember that I thought I was so clever and my mom was open to the idea that you could warm the car up faster (temperature in car not engine) by turning on the defroster or heater when it was cold and forcing the air through the system as opposed to waiting for the engine to warm and then turning on the defroster or heater. I was smiling on the inside. I felt clever, that my idea was considered and valuable, that I could make a contribution even at that age. I could matter, even then.

I am not exactly sure what happened in this journey, but I was told that I was regaining, reclaiming something from when I was 10, reclaiming my 10 year-old self. It happened to me, not through an effort on my part. I was asked how I felt in the car, driving down the road, sitting in the front seat, and I felt content and even still pretty happy and filled with possibility.

Although the joy and contentment were soon to end in my life, there seemed to be something important about me remembering that I had it then. There is some tie to yesterday's writing about what is lost along the way that can be re-claimed now as the wounds are healed and the layers of indoctrination and habituation are removed.

> ***You relinquish parts of yourself like turning in your clothes and accepting a uniform.***

Them: Yes, that is right. You have it right. This was an exercise for you to do what we were speaking of yesterday, going back to remember what you were like before much was lost. And this point in your life was among the very last times before your essence was lost. Up until this point you had more freedom and more joy and wonder than you would have again, until now. This was the end of the road in that sense, and we want you to remember yourself up until that point so you may find her again.

It is a process to return and remember and re-experience yourself in your purest state. In going back there can be pain, hurt, and anger over how things went and how you were influenced to lose yourself. While this may not be true for all of you to the degree it was true for JB, it is true for all to some degree.

The indoctrination to societal ways and familial ways requires a relinquishing of self.

When did yours fundamentally occur?

What were the biggest things you lost?

Although as we said yesterday your indoctrination into society begins prior to birth, there is a point at which it tips into a significant loss of self, where you can no longer keep essential pieces of yourself and be lauded by your family and society, and so you give in. You relinquish parts of yourself like turning in your clothes and accepting a uniform.

It is a sad moment for us, as your focus becomes what others want or expect from you. Your focus on your own sense of self and wonder for the world becomes dormant, hidden away in a cave, hoping to be found again someday.

Usually this period of dormancy lasts well into adulthood, until there are enough cracks in the societally proscribed life you have created that you go on a journey for new answers. What you find on the journey is a desire for self, a desire to reclaim your essence. This is the day we await, for in these times, all is possible again.

It is interesting to us that people tend to call this a mid-life (or other kind of) crisis, but to us it is an awakening from a drug-induced sleep. The drug was societal and familial acceptance. But as everyone finds out if they are open to it – the price of that acceptance is too high. The loss of self is too complete. And the opportunity of this life is lost.

You have a choice between following their lead or following your own heart and, fortunately or unfortunately, you cannot do both. One life must be chosen. Which will you choose?

For those of you ready for the journey back to yourselves, we are here. We will support you every step of the way. And to all of you, blessings. Amen.

Jeannie Bertoli

BREAKING INDOCTRINATION THROUGH CURIOSITY

Good morning. We are so glad you are here today. You are in a wonderful zone with us, growing and more open each week. It is so exciting to watch you, with curiosity and wonder, delve into this world with increasing trust and interest. The world is before you. Keep going.

Today we want to talk about curiosity. It is one of the things lost as you pay attention to what others want for you more than what you want for yourself.

The incentives for curiosity are fewer and fewer. There are certain parameters within which curiosity is still acceptable – within scientific research or new technologies. Within your personal lives, however, and in the process of how you live your lives, there is little acceptance.

We have given you examples before, but let us give you a few more beyond parameters you would find acceptable. What if someone wanted to eat with his/her toes, someone who was not handicapped in a way that necessitated that? Look at how difficult it would be for a man to wear a skirt, or heels, or make-up. And these are the tiniest of changes. It takes almost nothing for people to be considered 'weird' or 'odd'. This is by design.

By separating those who are acceptable from all 'others', the first group is treated as acceptable and the second is treated with disdain. This disdain, as dished out by all of the 'acceptables', takes a serious toll on the 'others' and gives them every incentive to get in-line and comply, to act within the incredibly narrow parameters that have been preset.

> *Curiosity is one of the things lost as you pay attention to what others want for you more than what you want for yourself.*

As you can tell this is disturbing to us, as it is such a strong force that only a very small minority dare go beyond it. Luckily, this is a time in history when many are seeing their lives as not working, and the systems around them as not working.

Most don't yet realize it as such, but that bargain they made was a rouse. They did not get what they were promised for giving up who they really are. And so the bargain is broken, and to a degree the spell therefore is broken. It is a short window (in our sense of time) before a 'strong' society will again assign rules for acceptable life.

Right now there is only this small crack where people may awaken, open their eyes, and see that even if they did get what was promised, it was a bad trade. What is lost in the trade is irreplaceable and essential.

So now, in this time of opportunity, one way to a new life is through curiosity. Re-awaken the five (or eight) year-old within you. Look at your world with eyes anew. Remember what it was like to wonder about everything – to open new doors constantly and draw and play and run and move your body.

All the things you tend to focus on now – technology, food, television, vices, work, obligations, schedules – did not exist. You wandered through woods or even through neighborhoods or stores – observing and absorbing – without the need to acquire things. Enjoy a walk in the woods without being so concerned about the bugs biting you or what time it is and when you need to be somewhere. Get lost in the beauty of a fire and the challenge of building it, knowing it is not about just enjoying it once built but what you can learn along the way. Curiosity is a way back to yourself. Stare at your dog while you lie on the floor.

Forget about all the things you 'need' to do. There is nothing you really need to do.

What do you choose to do?

Most of you are so very far within the confines of the proscribed life, including JB, that you need to re-claim wonder, curiosity, and fun. Even schedule it in if that will help. Schedule in two hours of not watching the clock and just wandering through life.

The other day, JB was awaiting an oil change on her car and so she spent an hour wandering through a mall with no agenda other than to buy some inexpensive sunglasses for her move. It was amazing the freedom she felt when there was nothing else she could do, no agenda for being productive, and she could just wander. The freedom and joy it brought her was really silly and reminded her how far she had come from the purity of just existing and experiencing life around her. And she does not even like malls.

Now for others of you, if you had been in that experience, you would have been looking to purchase (acquire) products and would have missed the point. The point was to experience the sounds and sights and people and products around – how the stores were set up, the colors – whatever piqued your interest, to just experience it. We invite you to go somewhere this week and wander without an agenda, without concern for time, and without ideas of acquisition. Just experience your world in a new way.

See if you can reconnect with the five year-old inside and simply be in curiosity.

Blessings to you all.

> *We invite you to go somewhere this week and wander without an agenda, without concern for time, and without ideas of acquisition. Just experience your world in a new way.*

BEGIN THE JOURNEY WITHIN

Well, good morning. Wow! It has been quite a few weeks, huh? You got your new car yesterday. We are so happy for you. We know you are very happy, or will be in the coming days, and that you will love the car and get many years of joy, comfort, and safety from it. It is the perfect car for you as you are, by nature, someone who greatly dislikes waste.

Not only did you get a great deal on the car, including on the extended warranty and saving lots of money on taxes by buying it before your move, but also you will save much by having a hybrid over the life of the car through gas and much less maintenance. You should write down all the maintenance tips you got from the guys because you already don't remember all of them.

We know you had a few bumpy moments yesterday with you getting misinformation consistently and needing to ask many people to get the correct information, but you did it and made all the right choices. Your choices were affirmed when, despite being packed and ready to leave, you easily found the title to your old car and got the cashier's check from the bank in less
than five minutes. The doors easily opened for you. How wonderful. Congratulations!

For us, the real joy was watching you stay aligned with us, feel your way through the process, and still be you. We smiled as you convinced the salesman to give you a nice water canteen and coffee mug since he couldn't give you more off the car. You combined the best in you with the alignment of the Universe. There may be a time when you have enough money that you want to be more generous with the dealership rather than bargaining so much, but this was not that day.

> *All of you may learn how to get in touch with your inner-wisdom and tap into 'other ways of knowing'.*

And you did it in a way that maintained relationships with these people such that they were hugging you on the way out the door and feeling good about you. That is also a big difference for you.

Congratulations, again!

Now on to other matters. There is much to be learned from this experience for all others. As JB has been learning to release and trust, so you too have that same path to follow if you decide you are ready for a new life. Not everyone will have an easy process to get a new car, but her process included two years of waiting and listening for the right opportunity. Your 'right' opportunities will be different. Your desires will be different.

What needs to be the same is the process of listening and aligning. This has been a long and incremental road for JB as it will be for most of you. Learning to turn within and become attuned to your own depth, well, it is a process, one that no one else really teaches you. All of you may learn how to get in touch with your inner-wisdom and tap into 'other ways of knowing'.

We love the phrase 'other ways of knowing'. It really captures the breadth of what we are talking about. There are other dimensions, other entities, other 'things' beyond your comprehension, with the limits of this form. You will never know all of it, but if you listen, you sense it. You sense, most of you, that something more is going on than you can see, hear or touch.

You know through science and technology things you could have never experienced without them. So too, there is much more in terms of other dimensions, other existences that are beyond your comprehension.

Although you may never grasp them while on earth, you can start down the path. You can come into relationship with the spiritual realm and learn what is in your capacity to learn.

By default, with the influences we have discussed (societal and familial and most religions), you do not come into direct relationship with spiritual dimensions. You do not leave the world of form and touch the Divine, especially in western cultures. And of course we are not talking about following anyone else's experience like church leaders who claim this privilege for themselves.

We are talking about you being in relationship with all that lies beyond here, in personal relationship. You each have the ability to tap into this, to reach through 'the veil' as some call it. This is not only for the scope of the 'woo woo', 'new age' people. It is for each of you. Each of you is from Spirit. You are one from the larger One. Right now you are distinct but still connected, and will again return to the whole.

This life is an experience for you. You get to 'experience' life in this manner with these characteristics, but they are not you...they do not define you.

They are simply one derivative of all that is possible, shoved into one form in one dimension. We know this will be difficult for many to understand, but we do not want you to take this one derivative in one form to be 'who you are'. You are not that simplistic or limited. You, again, are experiencing one derivative of all that is possible. And next time, you will experience a different derivative in possibly a different form with different rules of existence.

Think about that. It is time to go for today. Have a great day. Blessings to you all.

> *Each of you is from Spirit. You are one from the larger One. Right now you are distinct but still connected, and will again return to the whole.*

Wisdom Beyond Me

Jeannie Bertoli

SEEK "OTHER WAYS OF KNOWING"

Good morning. What a day, what a week it has been. We will say for everyone else out there that JB's little dog got a possible diagnosis of bone cancer that metastasized to her lungs and she was told if this was the case that her dog would have a brief and deeply painful end, imminently. So, she spent the day preparing to put her loved one down but never heard back to know if the diagnosis was correct. She will know today.

We are here to say that it is not what they think, which you will know. She is much better than you thought. She will be well for a while longer. She is not going to die soon and you will not have to put her down soon. She is not very well right now with some issues, especially in her left front shoulder, but we tell you to keep giving the treatments you have been and she will continue to progress over time. You must simply not be upset with setbacks, even serious ones. They are a part of the healing process and this is her life, at least for now.

So get a system together for her treatment with food, physical therapy, and pain management through medication and acupuncture. Get it set, then let it be and leave her to heal. Each day means little. It is weeks and months; just be with her and you will see. You spent much time in the past three months in misdiagnosis and inaccurate treatments. Now it is different. Give this three months and then reevaluate, but she does not have cancer and is not about to die. Know that.

JB Update: My Piccola was misdiagnosed and had no cancer and is now well and happy, though with periodic setbacks and issues.

> **You ride on the wings of angels and have no concerns.**

You are moving tomorrow and today is your last day here in this house, this city (Santa Fe, NM). Spend the day in peace. Go through your lists in calm and peace. Be well. Do not rush or stress. All is well. You will have a peaceful last day and get in the car tomorrow. Do not worry about anything. You have not heard from your new landlord. It is fine. Other things have not come through; they are fine.

You have no concerns, as you are taken care of. You ride on the wings of angels and have no concerns. Continue to trust us and allow life to unfold as it has. As it has, so it will continue to.

Your trip and your journey will be blessed. As you have long known, you and your dog will do very well and be much improved in your next location. And so it will be. Blessings to you child. We know you have been through much change. Continue to feel uplifted and carried into a wonderful future.

And now on to other matters. You had someone ask you the other day, someone who is intuitive, how he could do what you do. Your answer was interesting to put out to everyone. You said what is right – that this is a relationship that has developed over time. Although you were able to receive messages like this from the beginning, which we will address in a moment, your trust in, and listening to and following the messages has expanded. Therefore, so too has there been an expansion in what you receive.

This relationship grew as you increased our time together, were more consistent in spending that time together, and acted upon the guidance you received. Then you were available to see/feel/experience more of the Divine, and to co-create with us. The Divine within you matched the Divine outside of you. They were in alignment and in relationship and so could create together. Like that old television cartoon 'Power Twins', as they 'unite' and put their fists together, their power increases exponentially. It is like that.

We have the power of the Light of the Universe, and you have that somewhere within each of you too. And when you join… 'pow'. So his question was: How do you do this?

You begin doing this by sitting and listening – trying to listen from your heart and not your head. Ask questions and then await the answers.

Put on drumming, toning or other beautiful, soothing music to occupy your brain...and allow what comes. It is a process to find your way inside as you have been trained both to attend to your brain and emotions, and to attend to the outside world. Let us say that again. You have been trained to pay attention to two categories of things: your thoughts and feelings, and the outside world. You have spent your time trying to please them, serving them as faithful masters.

Now as you begin to live from a different place, go within to find your own Divinity, and then connect with the Divinity of the Universe. Connect with Divinity outside of yourself both through experiencing the Divinity in others and beginning a relationship with the more Universal Divinity (us) through 'other ways of knowing'.

You all have it in you to leave this dimension, to remember what you have experienced before. Seize that; express that. It is a way to an entirely new life, and planet and universe. Just imagine if everyone spent 30 minutes a day going within and experiencing pure light, pure truth, other dimensions? Imagine if that time was focused on things outside of sensory experience, outside of the ability of the form. What a life that would be. What different things you would manifest.

Continue forth now. Spread the word to all who have ears to hear. Many are ready for the simplicity of this message. Many know there is more and long for something, though they know not yet what it is – what it is, what to call it, or how to describe it. They know only that there is something – something either calling them or something missing. Those of you who are ready, begin the journey within, which is a journey to yourself and to us. And those of you who are ready, begin asking people, gently, if they feel something is calling them, something is missing. Ask them what it is...see what comes.

On your journey, blessings always. Amen.

> *Those of you who are ready, begin the journey within, which is a journey to yourself and to us.*

Jeannie Bertoli

ALIGN WITH THE RHYTHMS OF LIFE

Good morning. We are so glad you are here today. Today you are in your new location. You made it. You arrived safely yesterday and Piccola is already much improved. This was a situation where your health and hers would be greatly improved by simply by moving to this area, Santa Barbara, CA (and especially away from your old area). We knew that, but it made no sense to you, so you just had to trust us. You did and here you are. How could it possibly make sense that Pica's health would improve greatly overnight by moving 1,000 miles? It doesn't through the eyes of form, but it is nonetheless true. Blessings to you both.

Lately you have gotten so many validations for your sensing. You sensed that the housing situation here might not have been well-maintained, and you could not have been more right. And there have been many things with many people that you have sensed. The great news is that you are beginning to really trust your own sensing over the thoughts of others – keeping your own counsel rather than seeking the opinions of others.

While you will always want others input and care what others think, it is important for you to trust your own instincts;

you are growing in that. We are happy for you. Also this means you are sensing from a deeper, more aligned part of yourself rather than only using your brain and deductive reasoning. You have such an amazing brain that quickly synthesizes verbal and nonverbal information. While you are mostly correct in the conclusions you draw, it is not the place to come from for the matters you now deal with. Now you must continue to shift your focus to sensing information your brain does not receive. This is the realm of your new life.

> *Now you must continue to shift your focus to sensing information your brain does not receive. This is the realm of your new life.*

Of course your brain will still be incredibly useful in absorbing the information you get from Other Ways of Knowing and applying it to the life of form.

For example, if you get information about someone through your connection with us (with the Universe), you then still need your brain to decide how to discuss this with the person, if at all, and how to then proceed. You also need your brain for all other implementations, like business matters, relationship happiness, etc. So the two sources of information or tools work hand-in-hand.

You receive information from the depth of yourself, and then you come back to the world of form and use the tools from there (i.e. your brain and body) to implement what you know to be aligned with Life.

Wouldn't it be great if people capitalized Life the way they do God? Be aligned with Life. Seek the answers in Life. Live in love with Life! With that phrasing, there would be a shift away from an outside parental figure with all the answers to becoming a part of what you already are, seeking to be your true nature, aligned with all life, with Life.

Wow – that would be amazing.

As you know with the brief study of fractals you have done, what is true, is true for all nature, at all levels – the same processes happen to micro-organisms as happen on the largest scale. When you feel the rhythms of these ways, the rhythms of life, you may allow them to carry you through life like you are riding gently and easily on a cloud.

These rhythms exist within every cell of your body, and derivatives much smaller than that. And they exist with galaxies as well. There is no escaping them. The easiest and most joyful and peaceful life you will have is through aligning with them. Feel the pulls within your body, the same as the waves of the sea. Be in life in this way; be a part of it like another instrument in a symphony. The ways of life simply are – they are beyond you and not movable to anyone's desires.

If you make choices against the laws of nature, there will be a feedback loop to correct that choice. Time may be long or short, as Life is much slower moving then you imagine.

You strip the land, treat each other with violence and hatred, and there will be a corrective action. There is no other way. If you go against a loving heart and act from pain or greed, there will be corrective action. It can be no other way.

You may call this consequences or karma, but it is simply life coming back into homeostasis. When energy builds in one area to a pressure point, then an explosion happens, then a reparation and recovery period, and then calm again. This is a feedback loop.

It is true of systems at every level – from a single family to the geo-political. This basic law of systems happens within every animal system, elemental systems, etc.

We know this is much for you all to take in but we want to introduce you to the laws of nature within yourself so that you may begin to attend to them. Start to feel from a different place.

Notice Life guiding you and pulling you toward your nature. It is long since over-ridden in your lives so you must quiet those other influences to hear and feel it.

You may call it your instincts, or perhaps not. Only you can determine that. But it is a constant voice, a consistent call. Its rules do not change and it is never silent. Be with it as you will.

Blessings to you all.

> ***Start to feel from a different place. Notice Life guiding you and pulling you toward your nature. It is long since over-ridden in your lives so you must quiet those other influences to hear and feel it.***

Jeannie Bertoli

FOCUS ON YOU AND ASK SOME BIG QUESTIONS

Good morning. We are glad you are here with us today. Today is a low-key day. It is a day to re-group. You have had such days of change in the last week that you got stressed and overwhelmed. Now is the day to turn around and get grounded and begin the road back to health and strength. You listened and aligned in all the changes, but you did not maintain exercise and healthy eating. So it is time to reclaim those two things.

Now your feet are under you again and you may proceed. You found an apartment you may stay in as long as you wish. You will come into yourself now, very quickly becoming healthy and strong again. You asked for a personal trainer and got that information yesterday. He will be a good fit for you. Be honest and unembarrassed about your goals. It is your time. Let him help you get back a body that you love. You have so many of the tastes and habits and you need only re-enact them and all will fall into place quickly. We have no doubt that you will.

JB Update: This took me another year and a half to get together...choice and practice are always required, even when guidance and support come to our doorsteps.

We are excited for you to feel a huge uplift in how you feel about life in form. Health, strength, laughter, joy, happiness, and even love and sex are coming your way. We know you are happy about all of this, especially making connections with new friends and having people close to your heart in your local community again, but different. You will be forming different friendships now and the difference will be wonderful. They will be more heart-based and deeper. This is the change you have made in yourself and the opening you have created. Enjoy it. Blessings to you during this wonderful time.

> *You set up your life circumstances and they can always be altered with a good look in the mirror and courage.*

And now on to other matters. As we usually do, we will take off from our talk to JB and tell you all about taking time to regroup, contemplate, and re-decide about the directions, the trajectories in your life.

You have set up these trajectories and played them out each day, and this time of re-grouping is perfect for thinking about whether those decisions should continue, whether they are serving your highest good.

EXERCISE:

Ask yourself:
- *How does what you eat serve you?*
- *How does your job serve your higher good?*
- *How do your relationships serve your life's purpose?*

Look at the way you are living and ask yourselves what it says about you. Where does fear drive your decisions? Where do you hold yourself back out of a long-standing belief that should be re-examined? "I would _____ except _____." Fill in the blanks for yourself. "If not for _____, I would _____."

What is it you tell yourself? What self-limiting belief is holding you back? You hopefully know by now that it is all a lie you tell yourself, and is often an excuse not to face another issue or fear.

One of JB's lies is: I would travel more if I had more time off work or if I had more money. There are lots of people who take time off work that they 'don't have' and those who travel with little to no money.

So what is your reason if those weren't options? You needn't travel 'well' to travel. So what comes up now? Is it that you are tired and don't have the energy? If so, it is time to look at that. If it is something else, then it is time to look at that.

We encourage you to look at where you are holding yourself back. What is at the core of it? What we promise you is that you are at the core somewhere in there. You set up your life circumstances and they can always be altered with a good look in the mirror and courage. We want you to know that if you say 'I can't', it is only because of you and not another and not circumstances, for those are all projections you have placed in your life.

You took your job (and can always choose not to take it) and you chose your relationships (and can always choose other ones). We do not mean to push you but to invite you. There are many who are sick of the results they are getting, sick of not feeling like life is what they want it to be. Many of those are ready to take on responsibility for their lives so that they might change it. You cannot change a life over which you do not have power.

You cannot force your daughter, boss, employee, or spouse to live a certain way or act according to your wishes. But you can have that influence over yourself.

Isn't it interesting how much people try to control or manipulate the agendas/trajectories of others without taking that same charge in the one life where they get to choose everything?

EXERCISE:
- *What percent of your time do you think about the actions or lives of others, what they have done or should do, or why they did what they did?*
- *Examine a day and your thoughts throughout that day.*
- *Look at how much energy you spend on the lives of others compared to your own life – what they should or should not have said or done, their motivations, etc.*
- *This exercise can be incredibly powerful. Are you up for the challenge?*

Take the one life over which you have complete control and exert your influence there. Realize how much you do this with others as compared to yourself. You try to get others to do this or be that so that you don't have to change. Think about this. It is more prolific than we can describe. It is so big that we shall say nothing else. We invite you to consider this mind-blowing possibility. Where does it apply to you?

Blessings to you this day.

> *There are many who are sick of the results they are getting, sick of not feeling like life is what they want it to be. Many of those are ready to take on responsibility for their lives so that they might change it.*

Jeannie Bertoli

A DEATH OF THE SOUL

Good morning. Welcome back. We want to tell everyone that you have been very sick the last few days and have been completely incapacitated. We are glad you are better enough that you chose to come and be with us this morning. We honor you for that.

Do not worry that you have 'lost' anything – any momentum or time – by being unable to move for so long in your initial phase of living here. There is no timeframe. There is no missed opportunity. You will be able to engage and meet people and make friends when you are better and even more when you are well. You will have another very slow week. We ask you to honor that and not push beyond what your body is ready for, lest you fall ill again. You are doing it right now – listen to your body and honor its need for rest and recovery. You have been through so much change. Allow your body now to catch up through this time of it turning inward like a ball. Continue that and you will be well. And again, there is nothing lost, nothing missed. Listen and advance as is appropriate without thinking about what you 'should' be doing right now.

Now let us move on to other matters. The world is at a time of change right now. You can feel it in the air; you can sense it if you are aware. This is wonderful to us because the time of false security is up.

You all were marching like drones to the beat of fear and safety for so long that there was no opportunity to reach you. You had an impenetrable mindset. You might lose your job so you need to... You might get in a car accident so you need to... You might get divorced so you need to... Your child must graduate from college lest he/she... All these thoughts and many others are based on fears of what might happen.

> *Did you ever think that what would best serve your children is not money or security but you breaking out of conventionality and being unafraid?*

At the end of the day they are all based on the worst-case scenario: being in poverty and homeless, or having a devastating health crisis. And while obviously you do not seek any of those things, neither should your life be totally organized around their prevention. There is actually very little work, for most of you to whom we are speaking, that required you to not be in poverty, homeless, or have paralysis or other medical crises.

So you get all of your insurances, you wear helmets and seatbelts, and then you tie yourselves to 'secure' jobs and put money away for retirement and push your children to do the same – all based on the premise that 'we shall not be poor, homeless, or ill'. Then when things do happen that are not 'the way it's supposed to be', you feel cheated and devastated and wonder what you did wrong.

And 'things' do happen. You lose your job or your relationship or your child gets in trouble or sick. This is life, and life happens. You are not meant to be protected from these things. They are a part of life and come to show you yourself and teach you ways to grow and expand your consciousness.

Trading a life of adventure and exploration for one of safety does not truly insulate you from the events of life. You exchange your life for this, and they can all happen anyway. Instead you can live and experience and create, and still make enough money to not worry.

You give lip service to your values being about loving each other and wanting your children to be happy, but in fact you have focused your lives on preventing devastating crises. Most of you would never make the conscious choice to live a fear-based life, yet look at what you are doing.

How many of you are living the life of your dreams in every aspect of your life? If some and not the others, why the trade-off? There is no need to tie yourself to a miserable or even monotonous job to have a family. Your children do not 'need' what you think they need. Did you ever think that what would best serve your children is not money or security but you breaking out of conventionality and being unafraid?

It is fear that has you put them in the best schools to get in the best colleges to get them the best jobs so they have the least chance of screwing up their lives. Can you see that? Do not say this is out of love; it is not. That argument is an indoctrinated one.

If what you want for your children is a happy life that does not have poverty and homelessness, then they do not need all of this. Happiness is not a life without struggles, challenges, or crises.

How do you teach your children to be happy? Really...how? You are certainly, collectively doing a poor job of it right now in your culture. Spoiling them and coddling them does not make them happy. Giving them what they want does not make them happy for more than a moment. And getting them to make the sacrifices you made will not make them happy. How will you teach them to be happy?

When they are the most independent and creative, in their teenage years, you do all you can to squash them and get them to play by the rules. You bribe and cajole and beg and punish.

You call them rebellious when they are excited and impetuous. When they do not wish to comply, you reprimand them. What are you teaching them?

We hope there are some of you out there listening. The problem is that you so long ago cut out those parts of yourself and fell in line with societal expectations, that you do not even question passing that along.

You are cutting off the best in you, for no good reason. It is like cutting off a dog's ears or tail because people have told you that this is what is done with that breed. It is ridiculous. Even more so, you are nipping off creativity, joy, and expansion.

Get in line and get with the program of working all day and submitting to the will of others so that at night you may come home, perhaps have a drink to deal with the fact that you hate your day, deal with dinner and kids and house issues, and then do it all again.

If you think we are exaggerating, you are wrong. Far, far too many people live a life that closely matches that description. It is a life of slow death. It is a death of the soul. You can start to turn this around by looking at what you have killed in yourself, what you have relinquished in the name of being a good, fear-based societal member. What joy, passion, creativity, or fun can you reclaim? Do you even remember what used to make you happy?

We are not talking here about getting loaded on one drug or another – be it shopping, gambling, drugs, alcohol, or food. We are talking about what lights you up, makes you laugh, makes you feel good inside.

Reclaim this for yourself and encourage it in your children. How shocked they will be when your focus is not on them following the rules. What a different relationship you may have with them when this shifts.

We will leave you with that this day.

Blessings to you all.

> ***Do you even remember what used to make you happy?***

THE TIPPING POINT

Good morning. Welcome. We are glad you are here. We know you are not feeling well this morning and honor that you are continuing this process despite that. You will feel better today than you do right now but be reminded that you are still very weak and keep your expectations small. Getting a few things done is still wonderful and progressive. Be kind to yourself and gentle with yourself and accept reality rather than fighting it. Honor it and know it is as it is meant to be. Bow to it, accept it, and wonder with it – what can it be here for, what is it here to show you? All those answers are possible when you are not in resistance.

JB: My immediate answer is to slow down and allow, to be here and not to have any agenda, which feels very difficult. There are so many things I want to be doing and feel I 'need' to be doing.

Them: There is no rush on almost any of it. There are three things you must do this month that have a specific timeframe. And you will get them each done. And the rest of it you will be in and work on, for sure. But there is no need to worry. Be here now. Learn to exist in this state in this place, whatever that might be. You are being shown that step one is to slow down, be quiet, allow for life to be. When you are unwell, you rest. When you are weary and depleted, you rest. Listen and align...remember?

> ***We hope you can see what an opportunity point this is. With the slow and big changes occurring around you, the veneer of security has been breached.***

There is a reason you feel this way. If you feel it is to show you the need to slow down, to listen more rather than assert, that sounds right. The upheaval of the many changes associated with the move, the car, and the doggie drained you much and you needed to be replenished. So be it. Why fight it? Why make more of it than that? Be in it. Accept it and allow for it. Fighting it, resisting it does nothing but extend it. We will leave you with that.

Now on to other matters. We would like to continue our message about trapping yourselves without joy and passion in your society. We hope you can see what an opportunity point this is. With the slow and big changes occurring around you, the veneer of security has been breached. Companies that used to take care of you with lifetime health insurance and pensions now have turned those over to employees and made them 'opportunities' to self-fund. And then of course jobs themselves no longer are secure, even where they used to be most secure, like police, teachers, and government workers.

Whether you can see this or not, this is the best news you can get. We know it is scary for you to 'lose' your sense of security – but it was only a sense of security. Now that the curtain has been ripped away, you can see that the wizard is just some old, little, anxious guy running around. He is not wise or omnipotent or omniscient...he is society. Society sold you all a bill of goods and you bought into it because the results were great for a time, then very good, then good, then good enough. And now you have reached the tipping point where they are not good enough.

Imagine a time, let's say right after The Great Depression, when the comfort and security of a manufacturing job with a steady, consistent income that kept your family with a home and food was worth everything. Well of course, then it was a win-win and both parties could be grateful for it. Few would not have seen that trade as a great one.

But over the years, the corporations came in and made increasing profits at the expense of all others – most employees, customers, and the environment (including the soil, water, and animals). There became only one concern – generating the most money for the top few. This was not new in history but it is the most relevant trend for you all.

You made a trade that you thought was a win-win because you got security. And you didn't much consider what you were giving up because you had been indoctrinated to the ultimate need for security. But times have changed and many of you are not near the poverty line, and so the formula needs to be recalculated. Many of you are expending large amounts of money on frivolous things that the opportunity exists to ask why.

Why do I work this much? Why do I live and train my children to live in a fear-based, creativity-killing way? Why do I squash the dreams of us both? Could I live simply without all these extras and be happier? What am I counting on now to make me happy?

Can you see that the fear from previous generations about not having food and shelter may still drive security-based decisions when those conditions are no longer true for many of you?

The opportunity now exists for you to see the system that has been at play. The changes have been so incremental as not to cause too much of an uproar, not to create a total rebellion of the workforce. Many of you see what we mean. There is a hamster wheel before you – do you step into it today? Do you ask yourself: what am I doing? Is this a choice of passion and creativity and expansion, or one of fear and security and obligation? And please do not automatically say passion for your family chains you to a life of obligation.

That is rarely true and should be examined for its deep truth. You see that we keep nudging you about this subject, and it will continue because it is absolutely critical. Without you opening your eyes, well, nothing else is possible.

And what is possible, is simply amazing. We invite you to it.

Blessings to you this day.

> *You see that we keep nudging you about this subject, and it will continue because it is absolutely critical. Without you opening your eyes, well, nothing else is possible.*

ALL YOU CAN REALLY DO FOR OTHERS AND WHAT YOU CAN DO FOR YOURSELF

Good morning. We are glad you are here today. Today you got an image of your father's childhood home, of what it was like when he was three to five years old. It was a very different image than you thought ever existed – a home of peaceful cooperation and joy as your grandparents felt very blessed to have their family. In this moment, they felt as though they had made it through such difficult years and found what they were looking for. It was a wonderful moment in time.

And while it did not last as various stressors took their tolls on each of them and the marriage and then the children, you can know that this moment did also exist. We tell you this to tell you (all) that you never know. You don't know people's relationship past because you don't know most of their past. You cannot know everything and are not meant to know that much.

There is no reason for any of you to focus too much time or energy on other people's business or relationships. You cannot know them, even when you think you do, and you are not meant to. Your focus should be on your life, your dreams, and yes, your families and communities, but not in the way people often do it.

You do not need to hash out and advise, unless that counsel is sought. So much time and energy is spent telling stories time and again to get a reaction that makes you feel justified in your feelings or attempts to make you feel better. All of this to no end. When you do these things, it does not progress you in any way. Mostly what you can do for each other is not buy into each other's stories, especially the victim stories, and instead to support and encourage each other to go within, seek their own truth, and tell them you will stand beside them as they courageously face what they find.

> *Mostly what you can do for each other is not buy into each other's stories, especially the victim stories, and instead to support and encourage each other to go within, seek their own truth, and tell them you will stand beside them as they courageously face what they find.*

That is the most you can do, really do, for people. We are obviously talking about peers here and not children, though similar statements could be made about your children. The most you can truly do for them (beyond feed, shelter, and offer them some level of protection, and transportation) is to teach them to go within, find their own wisdom, trust the depth of that knowledge and support what they find in this and other dimensions, and then support them when they courageously face the information they found.

Knowing that this is the best you can do for others, you may keep your focus to that. It is a big switch from talking about people's stories to talking about that. We taught JB a way to make this transition in a curriculum we delivered through her last summer and she taught last fall. Instead of responding in the typical ways, you listen from a very caring place and ask questions like: If there was a message from the Universe in this situation, what do you think it was?

This is just one example; there are many more. There are whole ways to challenge yourself and truly be supportive of your human brothers and sisters by not buying into their stories of being mistreated and wronged by families, bosses, co-workers, or systems.

That curriculum will be the subject of JB's next book: For All Who Hunger: How to Leave Societal Influences Behind and Live the Life You're Meant to Live.

Your focus in your life should be on asking the deeper questions and knowing what your life is about while exploring and experiencing what this life of form has to offer. At this point, you will find yourself full of wounds and triggers that must be faced and healed. You must do this to truly enjoy your life from a place of purity and peace.

Peace comes through acceptance and allowance. Allow the flow of life to course right through you and be a part of life on its terms, without trying to exert your will on top of it.

The biggest way you all try to exert your will is trying to stop the river of life. You work really hard to get this goal or that element in your life, and then when you've created all the change you want, then you want life to totally stop and you just want to stay in that one perfect state. Education, check; profession, check; relationship, check; house, check; kids, check...now STOP, I'm done, this is what I want, don't change! Sound familiar?

Well, it's never going to happen. That is not the way life is. It continues to flow. Relationships that are 'perfect' one day are imperfect the next. Children who are compliant are then not. A school that was wonderful is then not. Jobs, families, friends, everything. Situations that you wanted to now be stable can then not be so.

You have all experienced this and often when those inevitabilities occur, you see them as hassles or annoyances to your smooth life. Well, we are here to tell you that they are not. They are more life coming in. They are not hassles to be handled but more information and experiences coming to be a part of your life. When you shift to seeing them that way, opportunities abound.

Stop wishing things would not change. Honeymoon phases in every situation end, and you see major flaws. What do you do then? Those things that you notice are there to show you pieces of you and help you clarify you, and those relationships. You may use them to turn inward and understand yourselves better. What most people do, however, is they focus on the 'thing' with the 'flaw' and never take that look at themselves to see what they are reacting to (or how or why).

All relationships have cycles. You cannot stop them; you can only decide how and who you will be within those cycles.

There is an opportunity here to shift. Do so with joy and you will find yourself.

We love you and will leave it there for today.

Blessings to you all.

RELEASE THE SEDIMENT

Good morning. We are glad you are with us this day. Today begins a real start of getting grounded here in California again. Your head is starting to come out of just sickness to think about and want to be productive on other matters. Try to get your taxes done today so you can send them to your tax guy. He loves you but will need some time as things are more complicated this year with employees and two states. It will not be as difficult as you imagine. Just sit down and see.

As for all other matters that were bothering you yesterday, you learned how important it is to deal with them to stay in peace. For the others, JB got a call and got lectured to by her new landlord's girlfriend with whom she has felt a rub since they met. This woman was trying to boss her around and control her and tell her self-interested half-truths. That kind of thing triggers JB, who does not allow that treatment. And in her pushing back rather than being run over, this woman rallied the landlord and his sister against JB. So the girlfriend called yesterday and said basically shut up and enjoy the apartment or find someone to replace yourself.

The good news is that uncomfortable circumstances are always good news.

When things come to shake you, it is always to teach you something. In this case there are a few lessons that are relevant to all of you.

First of all, there will always be people who do not like you and rise up against you. What you do in those situations is what speaks to your character. JB just keeping her personal power and not being run over by this woman created an escalation in the other woman. JB did not escalate or cause this situation. She only stood her ground. And this was the reaction.

> ***The good news is that uncomfortable circumstances are always good news.***

Now to you, JB. That is the situation and it is okay. As you find yourself getting angry or defensive, as you saw this morning in meditation, you need do a few things. First of all, simply breathe and come inside yourself. Do not hype up the feeling and get in a whole thought-emotion escalating cycle that keeps you in the same place.

Instead, breathe. Come inside yourself, keep breathing, and just allow the sediment to sift.

When a situation has shaken up the contents of the glass and everything is all cloudy, breathing and allowing will mean the water can still and the sediment fall to the bottom. This is the perfect analogy for you as you are choosing to release the sediment in your life, and in those moments it is all confused and involved.

When you allow for the quiet and breathe, the sediment drops to the floor of the glass and you rise above, for that is the way of it. That is what happens naturally. You all are made of light and will rise when you release the sediment. That sediment can be ego, wounds, habituation, culture, or just the nature of form. But your spirit is always light.

We are not saying that each of you must not act out of that sediment, but you, JB, have decided to live without it and be on a journey to releasing it as much as possible. This is for your own self- interest and desire to live in peace. This is the process that you may follow no matter the situation, people, or circumstances:

Come within,
find that centered place,
detach from the thinking/emotional cycle that keeps the glass shaking,
breathe,
and allow.

And in that allowance, the natural process of sediment resting and you rising will occur. When you try it for the first time in earnest, it will amaze you.

So the first thing to learn from this experience is this process for recovery and seeing what is sediment, so you may make a choice as to how to proceed. When you stay in the sediment, that is your choice. That is the vibration of many actions and dynamics, and that is fine. If you want joy and peace, you will be on a path to raising your vibration, for it is the only way to peace. There is no way to stay angry and defensive and reactive, and be in peace.

As you journey toward peace, you challenge and allow and release those sediments more and more. That is the way of it. If you feel deep within yourselves, many of you will feel the truth in this.

You cannot be in peace and have road rage. You cannot be in peace and be an addict. We mean to say the degree to which you are peaceful will be proportionally limited by these things. To be on a path to peace means looking at, challenging, and releasing the systems that hold those competing energies in place.

This situation was also brought to you to see that you, JB, do have triggers around people pushing you around. While you are quick to defend that, and of course, no one should have the power to push you around, you needn't have the violent reaction you do to it. You may simply stand your ground and internally laugh and stay in peace, knowing no one has power over you. You can simply say 'no' with no energy attached to it. Your reaction was much more indignant and self-righteous than this, though you still reacted far more peacefully than in times past.

So the other lesson here is to look at the last step or two you can make to have peace around this trigger point. You have had reasons, many of them, to defend yourself against attacks. But those reasons are gone. You are in a place of power beyond measure now and you need no defense against people and their words.

Live in yes and breathing and allowance…and nothing can go wrong. Nothing can touch you. Live in your truth. Live in creativity and love and expansion. Live without fear.

There is nothing here that can harm any of you, for to say it is so is to say things here matter more than they do. You matter far more than anything that will occur in this lifetime, in this form. It is like saying a piece of clothing matters. This sweater matters. And putting years of energy into that sweater. It doesn't matter. It will soon enough be gone and will never have really mattered.

Think about what does matter. And in this case what does matter is why this situation came to you, what it came to teach you, to show you. What a beautiful gift the Universe brought you. The messenger matters not, of course. And if she was not so offensive, you would not have spent this time to understand and learn. Blessings to you for that. Mahalo.

Go now and enjoy the day. We love you all.

> *If you want joy and peace, you will be on a path to raising your vibration, for it is the only way to peace. There is no way to stay angry and defensive and reactive, and be in peace.*

CONCLUSION

I hope you have enjoyed this material. I loved compiling it for you and rereading all the love and support that is out there for us all. I believe with all my heart that you can receive your own guidance and answers for all your questions about Life, and your life.

Blessings to you on your journey.

If you'd like to contact me to tell me your story or ask any questions, you may do so through my website: **www.DrBertoli.com**.

> *Live in your truth. Live in creativity and love and expansion. Live without fear.*

EPILOGUE
Next Steps

Well you have made it through the book... congratulations! I hope it has touched and moved you. I know without a doubt that we are all surrounded by some Universal system of support, whatever we might wish to name it. You, yes you, are supported and guided every moment of every day. The only thing you have to do is clear the way for that information to make it to your consciousness. You can do exactly what I have done, absolutely, unquestionably.

If you are ready to open that door, to feel the comfort of personal knowledge and guidance for your life, let me know. Even if you are just inspired or intrigued by these ideas, you may be interested in figuring out how to receive your own personal guidance. You can! Everyone can. I am clear on that. What I do is not just for me, but available to all.

Go to www.DrBertoli.com and click on Wisdom Beyond Me to get more information and free stuff (including videos). You can also contact me through the site to answer your questions or book me for speaking engagements.

Until I see you again...blessings!

- Jeannie Bertoli

www.ingramcontent.com/pod-product-compliance
Lightning Source LLC
Chambersburg PA
CBHW071650090426
42738CB00009B/1484